PRELIMINARY EXERCISES
IN COUNTERPOINT

11-3-75

Also by Arnold Schoenberg

FUNDAMENTALS OF MUSICAL COMPOSITION

★

edited by Erwin Stein

ARNOLD SCHOENBERG : LETTERS

ARNOLD SCHOENBERG

PRELIMINARY EXERCISES
IN COUNTERPOINT

EDITED
AND WITH A FOREWORD
BY
LEONARD STEIN

FABER AND FABER LTD
London

First published in 1963
by Faber and Faber Limited
24 Russell Square London WC1
First published in this edition 1970
Printed in Great Britain
by John Dickens & Co Ltd
Northampton
All rights reserved

SBN (cloth edition) 571 05464 1
SBN (paper edition) 571 09275 6

© *1963 by Gertrude Schoenberg*
Editor's Foreword © *Leonard Stein 1963*

CONDITIONS OF SALE

CONTENTS

IV. FOURTH SPECIES
Syncopated half notes and suspensions in upper and lower voices added to the cantus firmus

V. FIFTH SPECIES
Mixed notes added to the cantus firmus

VI. THE MINOR TONALITY

VII. FIRST COMPOSITIONAL APPLICATION: CADENCES WITHOUT *CANTUS FIRMUS*

VIII. SECOND COMPOSITIONAL APPLICATION: CADENCES TO VARIOUS REGIONS; MODULATION

PART II

SIMPLE COUNTERPOINT IN THREE VOICES

I. FIRST SPECIES

Cantus firmus *and two added voices in whole notes*

II. SECOND SPECIES

Two voices added to cantus firmus: *one in whole notes and one in half notes, or both in half notes.*

III. THIRD SPECIES

Addition of four quarter notes to a cantus firmus *and whole notes or half notes in the third voice*

IV. FOURTH SPECIES

Addition of syncopated half notes to a cantus firmus *and whole notes, half notes or quarter notes in the third voice*

EDITOR'S FOREWORD

THIS treatise on counterpoint had its inception in the counterpoint classes conducted by Arnold Schoenberg at the University of California, beginning in 1936. For these classes, in which it was my good fortune to participate, first as a student and later as Schoenberg's assistant, Schoenberg provided numerous examples illustrating all aspects of counterpoint, from the simplest treatment of the species to chorale prelude and fugue. Some of the examples were prepared specifically in advance of class meetings, but many more, in accordance with Schoenberg's usual pedagogical custom, were improvised on the spot in the classroom to illustrate special points as they occurred.

Schoenberg always liked to describe his method of working in the class as 'proceeding systematically', that is, trying every possible solution in turn. In the first species of counterpoint, for example, he systematically treated each note of the *cantus firmus* with every possible consonance—prime, octave, perfect fifth, third, and sixth—proceeding measure by measure while discussing the advantages and shortcomings of each combination. This procedure may be observed in its application in several instances in this text: see, for example, under Comment on Examples in Two Voices, First Species (p. 14), in Exs. 11 and 12, Ex. 21, and Ex. 27. Such a procedure does not have as its goal, as in many textbooks, the production of one or two 'perfect' examples according to certain aesthetic or stylistic considerations, but has the more practical aim of encouraging the student to discover for himself every *possible* solution or consideration of a given problem within ever-widening limits. It so happens that this exhaustive study of all possible means often produces situations where the student either meets a dead end and has to start all over again, or is forced to discover for himself ingenious solutions that otherwise might escape his attention. The ultimate result of this method is the acquisition of a discipline which enables the student to analyse thoroughly all problems that might arise, and gain possession of a sure technique which will make it possible for him to find solutions for most of these problems.

Such a didactic procedure is actually the outgrowth of several preceding works of Schoenberg, particularly the *Harmonielehre* (Universal-Edition, 1911; English edition, *Theory of Harmony*, Philosophical Library, 1948) and *Models for Beginners in Composition* (G. Schirmer, Inc., 1942). In the former work Schoenberg examines all possible combinations of chords and progressions, proceeding systematically and exhaustively, in order to find out what is feasible, what is less useful, and even what is downright impossible, too. In the *Models for Beginners* the author gradually develops the construction of two-, four- and eight-measure phrases and sentences out of the simplest possible material—broken chords derived from a single harmony—gradually adding features of embellishment, motivic repetition, and variation, combined with changing and substituting harmonies. Finally, by this accumulative and analytical method, eight-measure periods and sentences, three-part forms, minuets and scherzos are produced.

In a similar fashion, in the present book on counterpoint Schoenberg advances the student step by step, giving him, as he says in his own English in Preface I (see Appendix A), 'advice in more or less strict form which will be changed corresponding to a pedagogical point of view'. There he further states that counterpoint 'will not be considered as a theory, but as a method of training, and the foremost purpose of this method will be to teach the pupil so that he becomes able to use his knowledge later when he composes'.[1]

To the scholar or teacher first glancing through this book it will appear that the author has merely followed the practice of J. J. Fux in his *Gradus ad Parnassum* in the strict application of the *species* technique. However, it will soon become apparent that only the most tenuous relation exists between the two works, the former providing merely a point of departure, as it were, for Schoenberg goes far beyond the usual application of the species in many significant ways. First of all, Schoenberg's examples provide many more problems and situations than those encountered in traditional texts based on Fux. Secondly, discussions and criticisms in the form of *comment* appear at the end of each main section as a directive to the student himself to examine, criticize, and improve his own examples; they often incorporate alternatives for the improvement of certain difficulties.

In regard to content, the following treatments, if not entirely unique in a counterpoint text, also deviate to a greater or lesser extent from the practices of traditional *species* counterpoint. Nearly all of the examples are presented in the major and minor modes only.[2] Beyond the five traditional species Schoenberg also introduces exercises without *cantus firmus* under the heading of Compositional Application, in which are included cadences, modulations, imitations and canons, in two, three and four voices. His unique treatment of the minor mode and of modulation depends on *neutralization* (see Simple Counterpoint in Two Voices, Chapter VI, §§ 64 ff., and

---

[1] In another note in English about this book Schoenberg writes: 'I plan still a theoretical part. Here only the practical which is only necessary for educating the student.' It is true that the *Harmonielehre* pays as much attention to theoretical aspects as to practical ones. In its emphasis on the latter the present book bears more resemblance to the *Models for Beginners in Composition*, which contains a greater number of practical examples in proportion to the amount of theoretical explanation.

[2] Schoenberg's consideration of the modes in general may be found in § 58, footnote. The only examples of church modes occur among the canons in Ex. 88, although he also wrote many fugues in the modes which were to appear in a future volume.

Chapter VIII, §§ 96 ff.), a procedure which guarantees strict diatonic progression by preventing cross-relations and chromaticism, and presents, at the same time and in an unmistakable manner, a statement of tonality. In other words, accidentals are not applied in a haphazard manner and merely to avoid certain 'wrong' melodic intervals—such as the tritone—but in a more functional sense, to distinguish one tonality from another.[1]

The concept of *region*, as an enlargement of modulation, was introduced at a later time into this book by Schoenberg, after first appearing in both *Models for Beginners in Composition* (see Glossary, p. 14) and *Structural Functions of Harmony* (Chapter III), where it is considered as being derived from the principle of *monotonality*. In this context modulation is only to be considered in terms of movement to or from various regions of a single basic tonality. Later, *intermediary regions* are likewise introduced (Simple Counterpoint in Three Voices, Chapter VIII); 'Their purpose is usually that of emphasizing a contrast through their harmonic differences. This is achieved by using the characteristics of these regions more or less as if they themselves were basic tonalities' (see §§ 148 ff.).

It will readily be observed that despite its great departures from the strict methods of Fux, this book also takes advantage of two important virtues of the species method: (1) practice in different metrical relationships, i.e. proceeding systematically from note-against-note counterpoint to mixed species; and (2) the gradual widening of the possibilities of treating dissonances. Among the latter Schoenberg utilizes only the following types of dissonance, which adhere closely to classical practice and which he terms *conventionalized formulas* (see § 17): the passing note, the accented passing note, the cambiata, the suspension and the interrupted resolution of the suspension. Auxiliary notes rarely appear and other types of dissonances occur so seldom that they are mentioned specifically in the commentary, usually as the only way out of an impossible situation. The dissonances Schoenberg allows are considered sufficient to enable one to study thoroughly the treatment of dissonance within certain limits, limits which may be eventually widened as one acquires a greater understanding of their possibilities.

In melodic matters the author does not depart from the traditional practices stemming from sixteenth-century counterpoint, in which certain melodic leaps are proscribed. Thus no tritones are allowed, or skips beyond the perfect fifth except the octave. In addition, advice is given for the balancing of leaps by change of direction as well as for the avoidance of compound leaps, advice which also concurs with classical practice (see § 7, Melodic Voice Leading).

---

[1] The strict application of *neutralization* often causes considerable difficulties in some of the examples; this Schoenberg justifies out of pedagogical necessity in the early stages of counterpoint. See, particularly, the explanation in § 143. Previous statements on *neutralization* are to be found in the *Harmonielehre* and *Structural Functions of Harmony* (Williams and Norgate, 1954).

Careful attention is paid to the cadence throughout the book; it is first considered in the sections devoted to the Establishment of Tonality (§ 10 and § 11). Herein appears the only reference to harmonic procedure, with the insistence that only the *authentic* ending should be used. Schoenberg's views on the plagal cadence, as producing only a 'stylistic effect', are presented in § 81.

As mentioned at the beginning of this Foreword, the genesis of *Preliminary Exercises in Counterpoint* lay in the pedagogical work that Schoenberg found it necessary to provide for his American students who lacked sufficient background for advanced study in theory and composition. Along with this book on counterpoint several others were begun at about the same time, but only two, excluding his essays in *Style and Idea*,[1] were brought to completion—*Models for Beginners in Composition* and *Structural Functions of Harmony*. Others, such as the present one on counterpoint and another on the *Fundamentals of Musical Composition*, were left in various stages of completion at Schoenberg's death in 1951.[2]

The counterpoint book, herewith finally completed,[3] was actually begun in 1936 with the aid of Gerald Strang (a well-known American composer and, at present, chairman of the Music Department of San Fernando Valley State College in California). The main work on it got under way in 1942, in the midst of a busy schedule of composing, teaching, lecturing and writing articles. When nearly one-third of the book was completed and in a more-or-less definite form, its progress was halted by a severe illness suffered by Schoenberg in 1946. Soon afterwards I helped Schoenberg complete *Structural Functions of Harmony*, and then we resumed work sporadically on the counterpoint book from 1948 to 1950, a year before his death. By this time nearly all the examples had been written by Schoenberg, but the text of the latter two-thirds of the book was essentially that of a first draft. Schoenberg specifically requested that the present editor be responsible for placing the book, and also *Structural Functions*, in the hands of the publisher.

The *Preliminary Exercises in Counterpoint* entrusted to me has actually undergone the following revising and editing:

(1) An explanation of the last four chapters of the book (in Simple Counterpoint in Four Voices), where Schoenberg had provided examples but no text or 'comment'.
(2) The addition of some small illustrations to amplify the text, particularly in regard to the treatment of suspensions in three voices (§§ 121 ff. and §§ 128 ff.), where, in my opinion, certain intermediate steps leading to more complex treatment had been omitted. (3) Some slight changes in the order of presentation, especially in the

[1] Philosophical Library, 1950.
[2] For the complete listing of Schoenberg's works see Josef Rufer's *Das Werk Arnold Schönbergs*, Bären-reiter-Verlag, Kassel, 1959 (translated into English by Dika Newlin, and published by Faber and Faber in 1962 as *The Works of Arnold Schoenberg*, A catalogue of his compositions, writings, and paintings).
[3] Rufer lists four different dates on which Schoenberg was working on a counterpoint book—1911, 1926, 1936 and 1942 (see pp. 123-5 in *Das Werk Arnold Schönbergs*; English edition, pp. 135-6).

sections on modulation (Two Voices, Chapter VIII; Three Voices, Chapter VII; Four Voices, Chapter VII). (4) A few changes, for the sake of consistency, from the concept of *modulation* to that of *region*, in line with Schoenberg's introduction of the latter concept in *Models for Beginners in Composition* and in *Structural Functions of Harmony*. (5) The usual little corrections of examples to make them conform to the strict pedagogical procedure advocated by the author, but sometimes overlooked by 'the author as composer' (perhaps other such 'errors' may have slipped through as well— a challenge to the perceptive reader!). (6) A number of grammatical corrections in the text; although for a person who was writing in an adopted language acquired late in life it is most remarkable not only how 'correct' Schoenberg's English was, but also how striking and distinctive his literary style became in this language as well (for further confirmation see the essays in *Style and Idea*). It is a style that is often very condensed, but it is always clear and vivid. Where changes of word-order occur I have always tried to preserve the personal tone of Schoenberg's writing rather than attempt to polish up what some pedants may consider a 'rough' style.

Finally, it should be mentioned that *Preliminary Exercises*, by its very title, implies that the author intended to write further books on counterpoint. That he did is borne out by certain statements written by Schoenberg regarding the material to be included within such succeeding volumes.[1] For these volumes he had collected a considerable body of material, some of which he used in his advanced classes in counterpoint, including examples of chorale prelude, double counterpoint and fugue, both simple and complex. These items were apparently meant to appear in a second volume, while a third volume was to be concerned with counterpoint in composition from Bach to Schoenberg, with special emphasis on counterpoint in homophonic composition. In addition, Schoenberg composed many complicated and fascinating canons, which it is hoped may some day be made available as the testament of a great contrapuntist and teacher, and as a further inspiration to the music student, to whom he addressed himself when he wrote: 'To train the mind of the student, to give him possession of this sense of form and balance and of an understanding of musical logic—that is the main purpose of this present study.'[2]

My acknowledgements and thanks are due to Giles de la Mare and Donald Mitchell for their help in preparing this work for publication.

LEONARD STEIN, 1961

[1] See particularly a letter on this subject addressed to Josef Rufer in 1946 by Schoenberg, and reproduced in Rufer's *Das Werk Arnold Schönbergs*, pp. 124–5 (English edition, p. 136). Certain material pertaining to the contents of these projected volumes will also be found in Appendix B of this present book (p. 224).

[2] Quoted from footnote to § 17, p. 23.

§ 132. *Again, open parallel octaves and fifths require watchfullness. The rule given by ancient theorist is too strict as regards to hidden parallels. But almost every theorist admits that some if the hidden can not be avoided and some have been used by many great composer. These are tolerable for example*

hidden parallel octaves
those are inevitable

are there perhaps the worst case of hidden parallel octav

letters

it matter whether between outer or inner voices no

tolerable — — — —

passing

§ 133. *There occur emergencies when a student would not know how to obey one rule without violating another or renounce of something which might be a merit. In such cases this author has asked his students to mark such shortcomings, indicating thus that he was conscious*

Page of the draft for *Preliminary Exercises in Counterpoint* (see pp. 96–97)

PART I

SIMPLE COUNTERPOINT IN TWO VOICES

THE FIVE SPECIES IN MAJOR

I

FIRST SPECIES

Addition of an upper or lower voice to a given voice, called the cantus firmus
(CF), which will always consist of whole notes in this book.

RULES AND ADVICE: INTERVALS, CONSONANCES, AND DISSONANCES

§ **1.** To every tone of the *cantus firmus* (CF) there shall be added a consonant tone. Addition of consonant tones is only restricted by the requirements of correct voice leading.

§ **2.** The following relations between two tones are consonances (or consonant intervals):

(*a*) 1, the prime—this is not an interval, because both voices sing or play the same tone:

(*b*) 8, the octave—either above or below a tone:

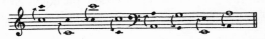

(*c*) 5, the fifth—which must be a perfect one—either above or below a tone:

and so not the diminished fifth (−5) which is a dissonance:

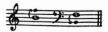

(*d*) 3, the third—major or minor, either above or below a tone:

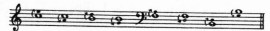

(*e*) 6, the sixth—major or minor, either above or below a tone:

§ 3. In the first species no dissonant interval shall be used. The treatment of the dissonance will be discussed later.

The following relations between two tones are dissonances:

(*a*) 2, the second—either above or below a tone:

(*b*) 7, the seventh—either above or below a tone:

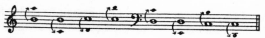

(*c*) 9, the ninth—either above or below a tone (a ninth is in fact a second plus an octave):

(*d*) 4, the fourth—either above or below a tone (the fourth is an imperfect consonance,[1] but in two voices it should be considered and treated as a dissonance):

(*e*) the augmented fourth (+4) and its inversion, the diminished fifth (−5), intervals which appear in the major scale between the fourth and seventh tones and vice versa:

[1] That is, it is only consonant under certain conditions.

(*f*) any other diminished and augmented intervals which may appear later, such as those in the minor scale.

Realize that all intervals, with the exception of primes and octaves, use different tones when below a given tone from those they use when above it. A fifth above *c* is *g*, but a fifth below *c* is *f*; and a third above *c* is *e*, while a third below *c* is *a*, etc.

§ **4.** Every interval retains its qualification as a consonance or dissonance respectively, even though that interval is augmented by one or more octaves:

THE VOICES AND THE CLEFS

§ **5.** The student will write his exercises for voices, and he will write them in the old clefs.[1] The voices which he will use are the same as those used in present-day mixed chorus: namely, soprano, alto, tenor, and bass.

[1] Contrapuntal exercises have for centuries been written in a traditional form—that in which the composers of former days wrote their compositions. Significantly, the three clefs—the *G*-clef, the *C*-clef and the *F*-clef—are related to one another as a tonic is related to its dominant and its subdominant:

All of these clefs were movable, that is, they could be placed on different lines, or even between two lines:

[*Footncte continued from p. 3*]

Many of these positions have become obsolete. In the eighteenth and nineteenth centuries, the treble

and bass clefs apart, only the soprano,   alto,   and tenor clefs

were to be found. But these still occur in vocal scores of Brahms, and even Wagner uses the tenor and alto clefs for soloists and choruses.

It is quite evident that today one could write contrapuntal exercises in treble and bass clefs, and for instruments—for a combination of strings or wind instruments, for instance, or even for piano—as well as for voices. But in this treatise the custom of writing for voices, and in C- and F-clefs only, is retained—not because it is traditional, but for two decisive reasons:

(1) Writing for voices reduces the number of errors a beginner will commit. The compass of the four voices mentioned above comprises a smaller number of tones than most combinations of instruments would make available. A lesser number of tones, a lesser number of *wrong* tones. Besides, it is easier to teach a beginner to write in a tolerable manner for voices than for instruments. Even in writing for the piano it may be difficult to keep the parts within the reach of two hands. But to write adequately for other instruments, one requires a knowledge of their technique, their individual compasses, and their dynamic potency, and last but not least—as many of them are transposing instruments—a knowledge of how to read them.

(2) Becoming thoroughly familiar with reading and writing C-clefs will help a student to read and play orchestral scores. Not only are viola and alto trombone written in the alto clef, and 'cello, bassoon, and trombone in the tenor clef for passages in their highest registers, but there is an additional advantage to be gained from the similarity of some clefs to some transpositions.

Although the soprano clef is not used for instruments in modern scores, it is useful for the reading of clarinet and trumpet in *A*, as the following shows:

In the same manner, the tenor clef is similar to the transposition of the bass-clarinet, B♭ horn and tuba in B♭, and it also helps in reading B♭ clarinet and B♭ trumpet, than which it is only an octave lower:

In a similar manner the alto clef resembles the *D* transposition of trumpet, clarinet, piccolo in *D* (which is an octave higher) and horn in *D* (which is an octave lower):

These clefs and their mutual relationships are shown in the following diagram:

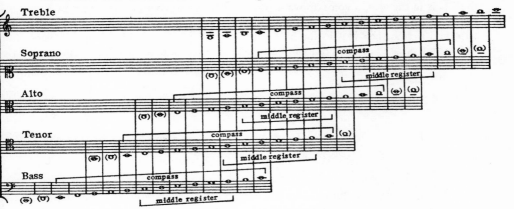

[*Footnote continued from p. 4*]

It must be added that the mezzo-soprano clef would help in reading horn in *F* and English horn (which is also in *F*) and trumpet in *F* (which is an octave higher):

A musician who is unable to read chamber music or full orchestral scores is one of a minor order. And even if he is a specialist, a virtuoso on one or more instruments, he resembles a juggler or a tight-rope walker rather than an artist. Therefore it should be recommended most emphatically that the student devote two to four weeks of painstaking practice to this problem alone. It will pay in the long run.

§ **6.** For his examples the student should always select two neighbouring voices. If the CF is in the alto, a voice above it will be in the soprano and a voice below it in the tenor—but not in the bass. If the CF is in the tenor, a voice above it will be in the alto, and a voice below it in the bass. In other words, the combinations of voices which may be used are: soprano and alto, alto and tenor, tenor and bass. Thus, the following combinations are excluded: soprano with tenor, soprano with bass, and alto with bass.

MELODIC VOICE LEADING

§ **7.** There is not much opportunity for writing 'real' melodies in contrapuntal exercises. A real melody requires a certain structural organization, and this imposes conditions which cannot be fulfilled in such exercises. However, the voices should be melodious or at least not unmelodious. This can be achieved by obeying most strictly the following advice:

(*a*) Every diminished or augmented interval should be avoided. In addition, as only the natural tones of a diatonic scale are to be used, chromatic progressions should be excluded likewise.

(*b*) In the seven tones of the diatonic scale there exists one augmented interval, the augmented fourth—called the *tritone*[1]—which in its inversion (in the descending scale) is a diminished fifth. It appears (as mentioned in § 3*e*) between the 4th and 7th tones of the diatonic scale:

This interval, the *tritone*, and its inversion should be strictly avoided.[2]

(*c*) Those progressions should be avoided where one or more tones are inserted between the 4th and 7th, or between the 7th and 4th tones of the scale. They shall be called *compound tritones*:

---

[1] So called because of the three whole-steps between the two tones. The symbol *tr* designates the tritone in the examples.

[2] This, and most of what follows, corresponds to the rules of 'strict counterpoint', as given by the old theorists and also by some contemporary ones. It should be mentioned that such rules are used here not for the purpose of imitating former styles, but entirely for pedagogical reasons. They prevent a beginner from committing the worst errors and gradually educate his ear to customary procedures as found in the music of the masters.

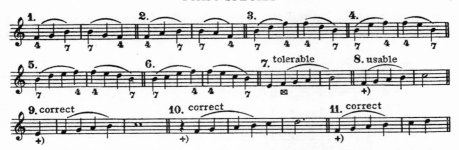

Of course, sections of a scale of five or six successive tones like those marked +) are usable, though the one marked ⊠ is perhaps only tolerable in an emergency—that is, if there is no better way of avoiding a problem.

(*d*) Strictly to be avoided are leaps of the dissonant intervals of a seventh, ninth, eleventh, etc.

(*e*) These intervals should also be avoided if they are produced by two successive leaps of intervals that are allowable, in the same direction. They then become *compound dissonant leaps*:

(*f*) Movement in one direction should not continue for too long a time. It should not go on for more than eight or nine notes, perhaps. After a leap one should avoid proceeding in the same direction, even stepwise. Instead, the leap should be balanced by movement in the opposite direction either stepwise or in leaps:

(*g*) The leap of a sixth should be avoided because in many cases it produces hidden 8s or 5s (discussed further in § 8). Theorists of traditional counterpoint allow the minor sixth upwards, but this also is better avoided. Of course, in emergency, if wrong parallels are avoided, both minor and major sixths may be used, both up and down:

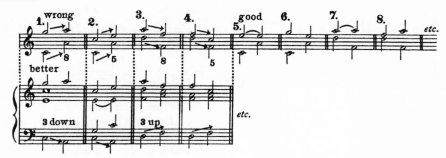

(*h*) Broken chords should be avoided as much as possible, for two reasons. First, they may express a harmony and thereby restrict the free movement of other voices in some cases. Second, they often give the impression of an accompaniment in homophonic style:

(*i*) Monotony is often produced through too frequent repetition of one tone or of a succession of several tones, and through remaining too long within the range of a fourth or a fifth:

(*j*) *Sequential repetitions*, that is, repetitions of a succession of tones at another degree (a second, third, fourth, etc., higher or lower), should also be avoided. They might produce a 'motif' whose obligations a beginner would be unable to meet:

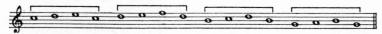

(*k*) The leap of an octave may be used in emergency if, for instance, the compass would have been exceeded, or if the voices would have been too close together or too far apart, otherwise. No leap over an octave is to be allowed:

(*l*) A good melody will mix leaps with stepwise movement and will not proceed too long in one direction. Change of direction will be obtained by a leap or stepwise movement in the opposite direction. Moving in 'waves' up and down will usually be the best procedure.

INDEPENDENCE OF THE VOICES

§ **8.** Since motivic combinations are beyond the concern of the beginner, the only rules demanding the interdependence of contrapuntal voices are these: that the voices should meet at certain points in comprehensible harmonies, and that together they should distinctly express the tonality. Otherwise they should be as independent as possible. (There is, of course, no real independence of content without motifs, which must be disregarded here. There still remains, however, independence of motion as regards direction, interval and rhythm.)

I. In writing for two or more voices there can occur three kinds of motion: parallel, contrary and oblique:

(*a*) *Parallel motion*, that is, movement in the same direction, is the least independent kind of voice leading. If it lasts for a considerable time one of the voices will offer the aspect of 'a shadow following him to whom it belongs'. But occasional parallel motion cannot be avoided, nor would it necessarily destroy independence.

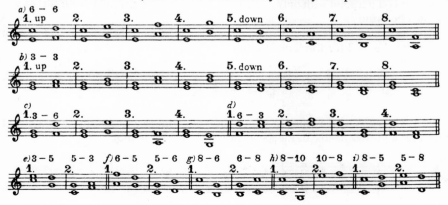

From his studies in harmony the student knows about parallel octaves (8s) and parallel fifths (5s). He also knows the difference between *open* and *hidden* (sometimes called *exposed* and *concealed*) parallels. *Open* parallel 8s and 5s—the parallel movement from an 8 to an 8 or from a 5 to a 5—must be strictly avoided. Parallel 8s destroy the independence of the parts. Against parallel 5s only tradition speaks. There is no physical or aesthetic reason for this interdict. *Hidden* parallels (8s or 5s produced by parallel movement from any other interval) are usually tolerable in three or more voices if they occur between middle voices, or if only one of the outer voices is involved.

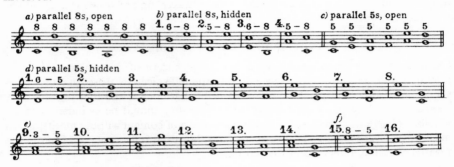

As the so-called 'horn octaves' and 'horn fifths' are almost unavoidable it has become customary to allow them to be used without restriction.

In simple counterpoint with only two voices, however, all other hidden parallel 8s and 5s must be avoided.

Parallel 3s and 6s are never wrong, though, as mentioned before, parallel motion should not be used for too long at a time.

(b) *Contrary motion* is that in which the voices move in opposite directions. It produces a greater degree of independence than parallel motion.

(c) *Oblique motion* is that in which one voice moves while the other remains stationary. This kind of movement cannot be used in the first species (unless one of the voices repeats a tone). It provides rhythmic independence at least.

In every piece of any length all three kinds of motion will be present: parallel, contrary and oblique motion.

par. cont. par. par.   obl.............   par. obl. cont. cont. cont. obl...................................cont.

II. Independence in the voices, whether there are two of them or more, depends not only on differences of motion but also on the manner in which they unite to form harmonies. Independence is reduced if they meet too often in primes or octaves, even in contrary motion. At least for the moment of their meeting they are not different enough. If only two voices are employed, triads cannot be produced. Though counterpoint is not supposed to be merely quasi-independent voice leading based on a harmonic scheme, the understanding of the harmonies produced by the incidental meeting of the voices helps to control its efficacy. But these incidental meetings of the voices must produce harmonies, and because of this the one voice added to a CF should as often as possible produce a third, or a sixth, or a fifth rather than a prime or an octave. Prime and octave should be reserved for the beginning, to express the tonality unequivocally, and for the end, to confirm it.

III. Independence of rhythm (not applicable in the first species) is produced in the second, third, fourth and fifth species by the use of smaller note values in the voices added to the long notes of the CF. But in cadences (see §§ 72 ff.) and modulations (see §§ 90 ff.) using mixed rhythms in both voices, a higher order of independence can be established. It would be too much to demand that a voice should move *only* when the second voice has a sustained note. But if one follows this principle, it often contributes greatly to real independence.

§ **9.** Crossing of voices must be avoided. Though crossing is not wrong it is in general too easy a way of dealing with problems. It is seldom necessary in these preliminary exercises, but later, in the more difficult exercises of contrapuntal composition, it may sometimes become unavoidable. Therefore it should be entirely avoided in these simple exercises and preserved for the more difficult ones. It should be considered a rule, then, in these preliminary exercises that a lower voice should never use a tone above a higher voice, and vice versa.

ESTABLISHMENT OF TONALITY

§ 10. Adherence to tonality is a basic and effective way of producing unity. In these preliminary exercises, as long as there is a CF and only tones of the diatonic scale are being used, the primary step towards achieving this is to begin and end with elements of the tonic (I) of the key in root position. This means that the lower voice will have no tone but the tonic, the first tone of the scale in either of these two places. But the upper voice can double this tone either at the prime or at the octave, or add—for preference—the fifth. The third may be used at the beginning, too, while at the end it should only appear if it permits some otherwise unattainable possibility.

If the CF is in an upper voice the lower voice can only double the tonic at the prime or the octave.

§ 11. The next-to-last (penultimate) tone will always be selected from the tones of the dominant chord (V), as in (a) below, or from the tones of the VII degree, as in (b). The leading tone (the 7th tone of the scale) should appear there, if possible. The lower voice may also use the root of the dominant (as in (a) 1 and (c)), but never the root of

IV, which is identical with the diminished fifth of VII (see (*d*)). In addition the forms in (*e*) must be excluded:

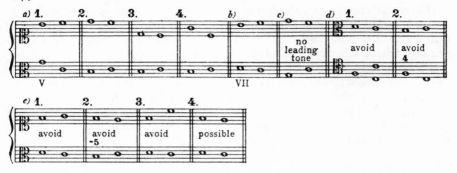

ADVICE AND DIRECTIONS FOR THE FIRST SPECIES

§ 12. If it is to remain within the compass of the voices, the CF must sometimes be transposed to another key (as in Exs. 2 and 3).[1] As to the question of the combinations of voices to be used in two-voice counterpoint, remember the advice given in § 6.

§ 13. The eight CFs presented in Ex. 9 contain progressions which the student has been asked to avoid. But they are made up in such a way as to include every possible step.

In two-voice writing the CF can be written in the centre of a sheet of music paper, and the upper voices added in the staves above the CF and the lower ones in the staves below. This is done here. The added voices *only* have to conform to the CF, together with which they build up two-voice combinations. No pair of added voices should conform with one another (see Ex. 1).

§ 14. A student must become familiar with all the keys. To achieve this goal he is urged to practise every new assignment first in *C* major, and afterwards in at least two to four other keys. In this manner the student will have employed all the twelve keys in a short time.

Further, it is necessary to change the CF frequently. Each CF offers different problems. Solving them will help the student to become acquainted with the great number of ways in which melodious voices can be added to intricate successions of three and more tones of the CF. The experience thus acquired will gradually accumulate in the mind of the student, and so he will be able to remember with ease 'formulas' which fit, and select the best one.

[1] Examples 1–9 at end of chapter (pp. 17–21).

COMMENT ON EXAMPLES IN FIRST SPECIES, EXS. 1–9[1]

The examples presented in this treatise are not made to convey beauty or perfection. On the contrary, procedures frequently appear which a student should avoid, so that their errors or shortcomings may be discussed. Problems are purposely introduced, and sometimes a satisfactory solution to them is impossible.

It is always advisable to plan an exercise a little in advance, and to ask which two or three tones could possibly follow a given one. Planning is almost imperative for the ending. There are often only a few possibilities, and one is then forced to shift a voice into a register admitting of melodious connexion with the preconceived ending. The penultimate tone of a CF will bring in the 2nd, 7th or 5th tone of the scale. The only possibilities then for the added voice are these:

It is best to proceed systematically, trying first as many examples as possible which begin with the prime and then examples beginning with 8, 5 and 3.

Since to every tone of the CF 1, 8, 5, 3 or 6 can be added, and since after such tones different continuations are possible, there is ample opportunity for variation. But it must be admitted that the severe restrictions at this stage make it almost impossible to write many examples which do not violate one rule or another. It is almost like the children's song which says: 'You may hang your clothes on a hickory limb but don't go near the water.' However, in spite of this it pays to try everything. There is the possibility of discriminating between greater and lesser 'sins'. And a merit might even make a rather serious violation pardonable—after all, the student is not going to publish his exercises!

Among such lesser sins might be an occasional succession of the tones of a broken chord; or a long progression in one direction, even when a leap precedes or follows it; or a succession of leaps, provided it is compensated for by a certain merit, such as the adding of a tone to the CF which could not be introduced otherwise. Such cases will appear more frequently in the species following after this one.

It is not wrong to use the same tone twice in succession. As there is no movement at

[1] The examples will come at the end of each chapter following the Comment on Examples.

all there is also no wrong movement. But, of course, it is more interesting if the melody changes with every tone of the CF.

Intermittent parallel 8s or 5s (often called 'afterbeating' or 'non-consecutive') like those, for example, in 4*d*, 4*f*, 4*g* and 5*d*, should be avoided. Even if another harmony or interval is inserted between two incidental meetings in 8s (or primes) or 5s, they are considered almost the same as open parallels. Intermittent parallels should be avoided as far as possible, at least in two- and three-voice counterpoint, even if the two voices move in contrary motion to the second perfect consonance. Nevertheless, in the diary of Beethoven there is a note saying that when one of the voices makes a leap of a fourth or a fifth, intermittent parallels may then be allowed. This would permit their use in the following instances, where there are such leaps and where the second 8 or 5 is approached by contrary motion, too.

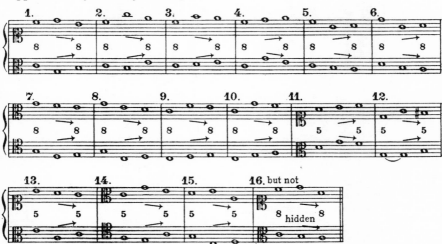

Entering into a prime or an octave is, of course, one of the possibilities in accompanying a CF, and so far it is allowable. But as it fails to add a harmony to the CF (as a 5, a 3 or a 6 does), it should only be done if it serves a purpose. For instance, in 1*k* at (+), the 8 allows the introduction of the 5, *c*, in contrary motion. The same is true in 4*d*, *g*, 5*c*, *h*, and many other examples. Sometimes it is not necessary—for example, in 4*b* and 4*f*—but may be excused since it produces a different melodic line.

The monotonous repetition in 4*i* could be avoided if the first three measures were done this way:

The tritone in *4e* (*tr*) and the monotonous repetition of the *g* can be avoided by going to *c* in ms. 5.

The intermittent 5s in *4g* can be corrected as in ms. 6 of the following:

EXPLANATION OF MARKS AND ABBREVIATIONS IN EXAMPLES

8 – – – 8	means open or intermittent parallel 8s.
5 – – – 5	,, open or intermittent parallel 5s.
↘8 ↗5, etc.	,, hidden 8s or 5s.
tr (tr)	,, tritone.
‾‾‾(7)‾‾‾	,, compound tritone.
⌢⌢⌢	,, compound 7, 9, 11, etc.
	,, two or more leaps in the same direction, *or* an ascending leap following ascending steps, a descending leap following descending steps.
⌇⌇⌇	,, unmelodious progression.
⌃⌄⌃	,, too many leaps.
6 – 6 – 6 – 6 3 – 3 – 3 – 3	,, too many parallel 6s or 3s consecutively.
br. ch.	,, broken chord.
rep.	,, repetition.
mon.	,, monotonous.
seq.	,, sequence or sequential repetition.
✗ ✗ ✗	,, note struck out for violating one of the rules.

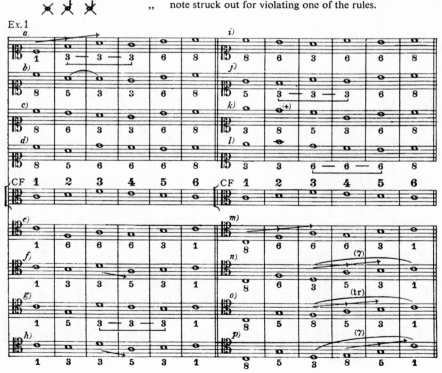

Ex. 2

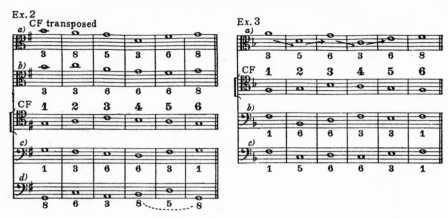

Ex. 3

Ex. 4

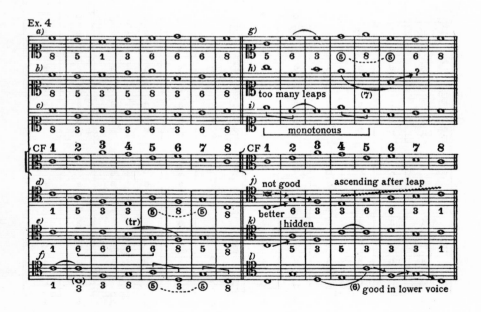

Ex. 5

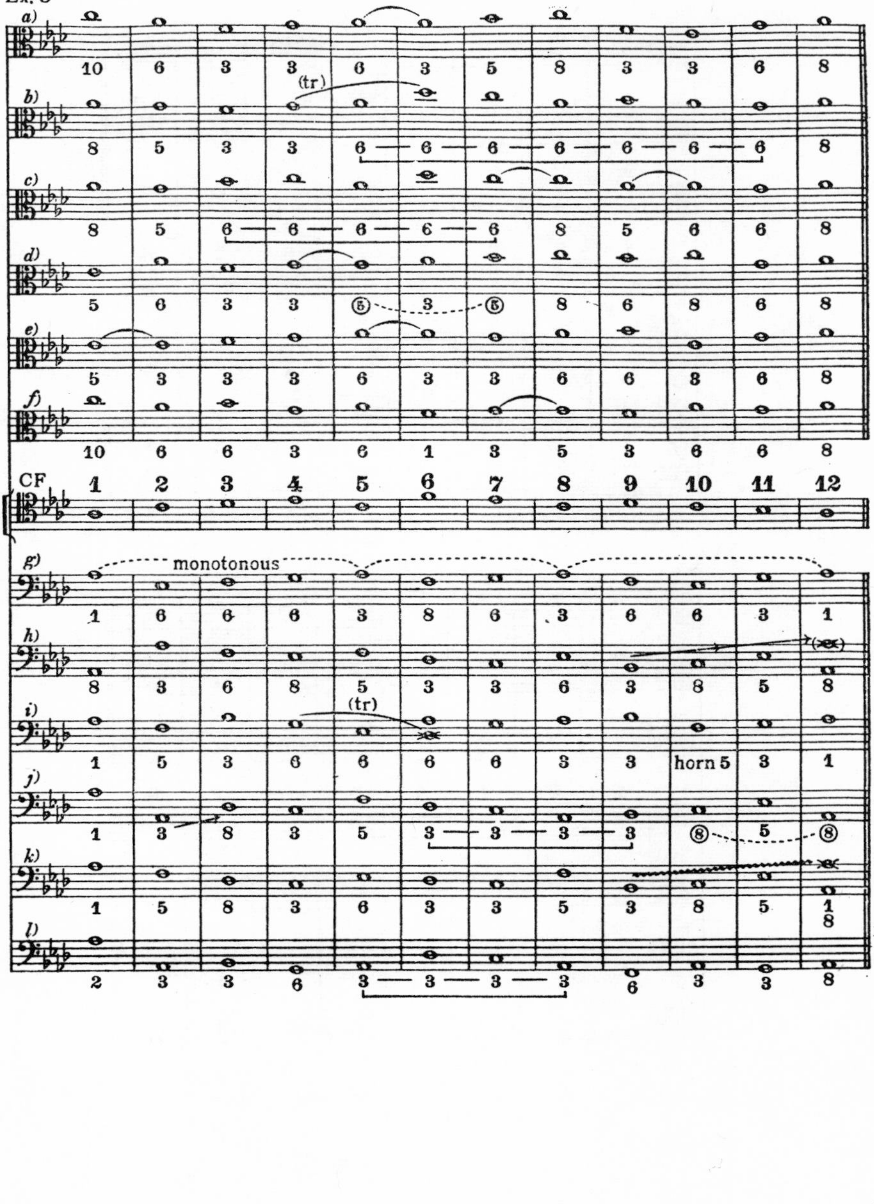
a)
10 6 3 3 6 3 5 8 3 3 6 8
(tr)
b)
8 5 3 3 6 6 6 6 6 6 6 8
c)
8 5 6 6 6 6 6 8 5 6 6 8
d)
5 6 3 3 5 3 5 8 6 8 6 8
e)
5 3 3 3 6 3 3 6 6 3 6 8
f)
10 6 6 3 6 1 3 5 3 6 6 8
CF
1 2 3 4 5 6 7 8 9 10 11 12
g)
monotonous
1 6 6 6 3 8 6 3 6 6 3 1
h)
8 3 6 8 5 3 3 6 3 8 5 8
(tr)
i)
1 5 3 6 6 6 6 3 3 horn 5 3 1
j)
1 3 8 3 5 3 3 3 3 8 5 8
k)
1 5 8 3 6 3 3 5 3 8 5 1 8
l)
2 3 3 6 3 3 3 3 6 3 3 8

* See Ex. 9

Ex. 8

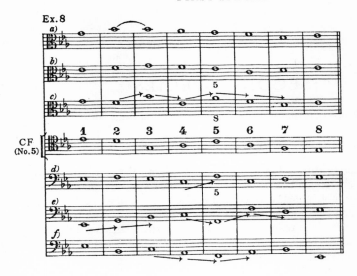

Ex. 9

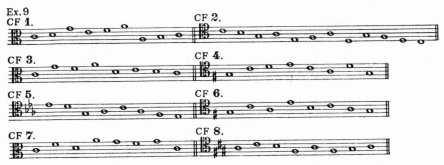

II

SECOND SPECIES

Addition of an upper or lower voice in half notes to the cantus firmus

ADVICE AND DIRECTIONS

§ **15.** If a whole note is divided in two (or four or eight), the first note in each pair of notes becomes an accented or *strong* beat, while the second remains unaccented as a *weak* beat. If the whole note is divided in three (or six), the first of every three notes is an accented *strong* beat, while the next two are unaccented *weak* beats. The first beat in every measure is the main accented beat, and strong beats within a measure are a little less accented; beats within a measure are only accented if the part to which they belong is subdivided.

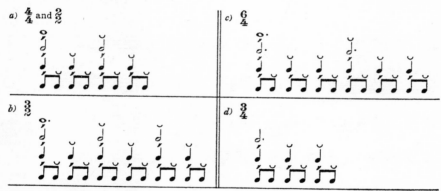

✔ means accented, ‿ means unaccented

§ **16.** There is a difference in the treatment of strong and weak beats as regards the use of consonances and dissonances. *Consonances* (1, 8, 5, 3, 6) can be used freely on strong and weak beats. *Dissonances*, however, shall be used only if advice has been given for their application, and only in accordance with such advice.

§ **17.** As progress is made from the simplest to more complicated cases, there will be presented many approaches to the *treatment of the dissonance*; the dissonances used will always be explicable in terms of certain *conventionalized formulas*. These formulas consist of successions of notes appearing in a definite order, metrical position and harmonic relation, which have been proved suitable, through centuries of use, for a smooth introduction of dissonances.[1]

THE FIRST CONVENTIONALIZED FORMULA: THE PASSING NOTE

§ **18.** The *passing note* (marked + in the examples) is a dissonance in a formula of three notes. The first and last of these three notes must be consonances a third apart, and must be placed on strong beats. The middle note between these two consonances, placed on a weak beat, is a dissonance. The whole formula forms part of a scale line moving either up or down.

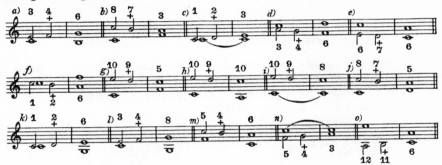

[1] The difference between consonances and dissonances is, as this writer has stated, only one of degree. Consonances appear among the first overtones, while dissonances only appear later. The first overtones have a greater similarity to the basic tone. Due to their greater distance from the basic tone the similarity of the dissonances is more distant (see Schoenberg, *Harmonielehre*). Usually this difference is also explained by the difference in the ratio of the vibration numbers. These ratios are simpler for consonances (1:1 for the prime, 1:2 for the octave, 2:3 for the fifth, 3:4 for the fourth, 4:5 for the major third, etc.); and more complicated for the dissonances (15:16 for the minor second, 9:10 for the major second, 45:64 for the diminished fifth, etc.).

The development of musical theories has certainly been influenced by these physical and mathematical facts. But the development of harmony—and counterpoint—took place under the influence of musical material, the tone and its overtones. Thus the history of music could be traced to the gradual emancipation of the dissonance. In early music dissonances appeared but seldom, and were treated with the greatest of caution. Such treatment led to the production and application of formulas which more and more frequent usage finally made conventional. At the beginning of such a formula the trained ear anticipated its further course; it came to expect the resolution of a dissonance in a conventional way, at the instant of its entrance.

To many a student this treatment must seem antiquated, and the student is right if he wonders whether there is a bridge between this style and the harmony of a Bach, a Schubert, a Wagner, and a Debussy, and that of post-Wagnerian composers. There is such a bridge, and to enter and to traverse it will give him much less difficulty than he imagines. But advanced harmonic techniques will only benefit him fully if a sense of balance and form, and an understanding of musical logic, enable him to control his ideas. A composer is, of course, directed by his inspiration. But he must not be the slave of his ideas; rather he must be their master.

To train the mind of the student, to give him possession of this sense of form and balance and of an understanding of musical logic—that is the main purpose of this present study.

§ **19.** Sometimes such a note will not be dissonant:

These examples are correct, but the middle notes here do not deserve to be called real passing notes. In three voices, however, the same notes might be real passing notes.

THE ENDING IN SECOND SPECIES

§ **20.** The ending in second species requires some discussion. The student will find out that if the CF ends 2–1, the penultimate tone in the upper voice can only be the leading tone (7th tone of the major scale). There remains only one possibility for the penultimate measure: 6th to 7th to 8th tone:

§ **21.** In the lower voice, however, there are several possibilities:

§ **22.** But it is quite different if the leading tone or 5th tone is the penultimate tone in the CF:

§ 23. The first tone in the upper voice must be none other than 1, 8, 5 or 3. The sixth would not express the tonality incontrovertibly. In the lower voice only 1 or 8 can be used at the beginning.

COMMENT ON EXAMPLES IN SECOND SPECIES, EXS. 10–18

Ex. 10 presents a few voices using only consonant tones. They are stiff, include too many leaps, and contain many broken chords.

Ex. 11 displays systematically all the melodic intervals which can possibly occur in a CF. Ex. 12 then explores systematically above and below three of these intervals the possibilities for the application of the formula of the passing note. It may be recommended that the student try the other intervals also in the same manner, beginning with 1 or 8 and moving up and down, and checking the other three consonances, 5, 3 and 6, afterwards. It pays the student to do this because he will then know at a glance whether a passing note can be used, and, if one can be used, which one.

In Exs. 13 to 18 both consonances and passing dissonances are used. 13*c* and *d* are very bad. One could excuse their faults individually, but so many transgressions could not be balanced out, even by some merits.

The monotony in 13*e* could easily be corrected in this manner:

A sequence like that in mss. 9–10 of 13*m*, should be avoided. Sequential repetitions assume to a certain degree a motivic significance, thus producing problems a beginner had better avoid.

The long leap after the long descending line in 14*g* is certainly passable, since otherwise the melody is correct. But the five successive leaps in mss. 5–7 are intolerable. They could be corrected as follows:

The broken chord form in 14*i* is tolerable as a means of reaching the tone *c* in ms. 3, which otherwise would be difficult to introduce. The *d* in ms. 3 of 14*k* is introduced satisfactorily in a similar way.

An attempt to use all the possible consonances and passing dissonances on each beat is illustrated in the lower voices of Ex. 15, mss. 2–4. The student should try the same systematically; it is of great value.

Many of the examples begin after a half note rest. This is necessary for the introduction of certain intervals, as for instance in 15*l*, ms. 2, where it would be difficult to introduce the third in a better way than through an octave leap.

Some of the examples (in Exs. 15 and 16) use a whole note (at ⊕) in their penultimate measure, thus interrupting the course of the half notes. This can be done in exceptional cases, but only at this point, never in the middle of an example.

The alto in ms. 3 of 16*b* leaps an octave because it can only reach the *f♯* in ms. 4, the octave to the CF, in contrary motion. And it is necessary for it to arrive at the *f♯* in order to be able to move in contrary motion to *d* in ms. 5, the fifth above the CF. Such factors determine the contour of the melody in many cases.

Exs. 17 and 18 illustrate possible treatments of two short CFs whose penultimate tones are, respectively, the 7th and the 5th tones of the scale.

Ex. 13

Ex. 13 (cont.)

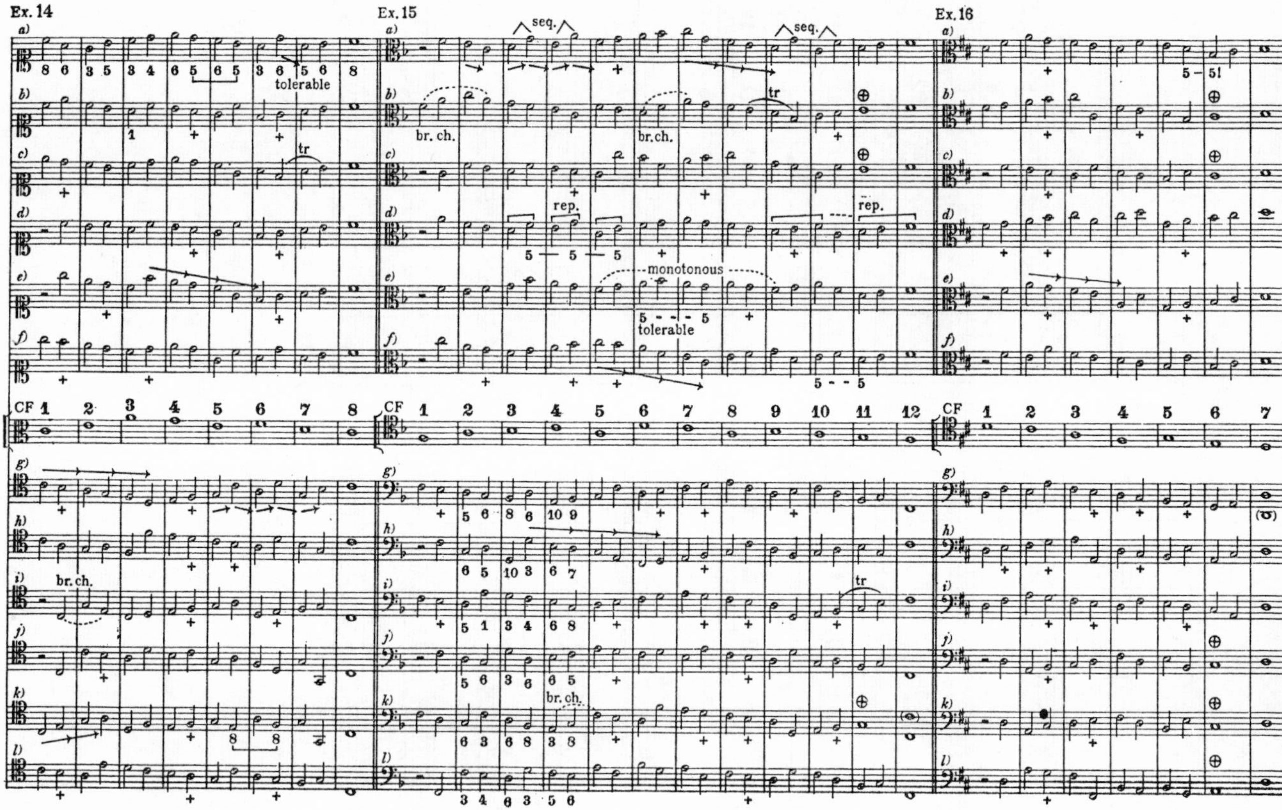
Ex. 14
Ex. 15
Ex. 16
seq.
tolerable
br. ch.
tr
rep.
monotonous
CF

III

THIRD SPECIES

Addition of an upper or lower voice in quarter notes to the cantus firmus

§ **24.** As has already been mentioned in § 15, the subdivision of every half note into two quarter notes gives an accent to the first and third beats in a 4/4 measure. The second and fourth beats will be weak beats and unaccented.

§ **25.** Consonances can be used on all four beats.

§ **26.** Dissonances in the form of passing notes can be used on the weak beats as in the first conventionalized formula; they must be preceded and followed by consonances.

§ **27.** This admits of the following distribution of consonances and dissonances:

Beat	1st	2nd	3rd	4th
(a)	cons.	cons.	cons.	cons.
(b)	cons.	diss.	cons.	cons.
(c)	cons.	cons.	cons.	diss.
(d)	cons.	diss.	cons.	diss.

§ **28.** Obviously these examples are stiff, even if they are not incorrect. But there is no reason why one should use any one of these four schemes exclusively in an example. On the contrary, one uses passing notes in every possible way when they help to make the melody more fluent. This is illustrated in Exs. 19 and 20.

§ **29.** The examples also become more fluent through the use of the second conventionalized formula, the *cambiata*. The cambiata is a formula consisting of five notes. Three of them must be consonances, and one or two may be dissonances. The first and fifth notes must be placed on strong beats (first or third quarter notes) and must be consonances. These, therefore, are the possible distributions of consonances (c) and dissonances (d) in terms of the four beats of a measure:

beats:	1	2	3	4	1		beats:	3	4	1	2	3
(a)	c	c	c	d	c		(g)	c	c	c	d	c
(b)	c	d	d	c	c		(h)	c	d	d	c	c
(c)	c	c	d	c	c		(i)	c	c	d	c	c
(d)	c	c	d	d	c		(j)	c	c	d	d	c
(e)	c	d	c	c	c		(k)	c	d	c	c	c
(f)	c	d	c	d	c		(l)	c	d	c	d	c

§ **30.** The cambiata appears in two forms: (a) *descending*, when the first note is one step higher than the last; (b) *ascending*, the inversion of the foregoing, when the first note is one step lower than the last.

The succession of the notes in the cambiata is definite and unchangeable.

In the descending form the second note is a second lower, and it is followed by a leap of a third down; there is then an ascent of two steps in the opposite direction, concluding the formula.

In the ascending form the direction of every interval is reversed: after a step up, there is a leap of a third up, then the next two steps go in the opposite direction, down to the concluding fifth note.

§ **31.** As with the passing note the student should check these formulas against every interval of a CF (see Exs. 11 and 12). In Ex. 21 only four intervals of a CF are examined.

---

[1] Often called 'Nota Cambiata' or 'Fuxsche Wechselnote', a changing note figure described by the theorist J. J. Fux.

The student should check the remaining intervals in the same manner, beginning with 1 (8), 5, 3 (10) and 6, and using descending and ascending cambiatas from both the first and the third beats. Some of the cambiatas are marked questionable (?) because of intermittent 8s or 5s. They may only be used in two-voice counterpoint if there is no other way out of a problem. In three-voice counterpoint, however, if one of the voices is a middle voice, they are admissible.

§ 32. Some forms are to be excluded because the ending is a diminished fifth (−5):

But even if this example were put into *G* major, and the last tone were *f*♯, it still would not correct the 5s between the beginning and the ending. This cambiata would still remain in the category of questionable applications like these:

However, in counterpoint with three voices the diminished fifth (and also the augmented fourth) becomes admissible, as will be discussed later:

In the examples the cambiata is marked with brackets: ⌐⌐. The student should do this too in order to become conscious of the correctness of the dissonances he uses.

PASSING NOTE ON THE STRONG BEAT

§ 33. The passing note may occasionally change its metrical position provided it is surrounded by consonances and is the middle note in the interval of a third. The consonances may thus be placed on weak beats 2 and 4, and the dissonances on strong beats 1 and 3. It should be mentioned, however, that theorists of traditional counterpoint forbade the passing dissonance on the first beat (as in (*b*)), and it will generally be avoided in our exercises as well.

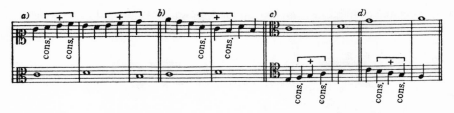

THE ENDING IN THIRD SPECIES

§ 34. The ending again requires discussion. The student will easily discover that there is only one melody in the upper voice in the penultimate measure which does not violate the rules (that which is used in ms. 7 of Exs. 19 and 22) when the CF uses the descending 2–1 ending.

In Ex. 23 several different endings are tried. Those marked ▱ in 23*d*, *e*, *f* and *g* are allowed by Fux though they contain intermittent 8s. They had better be used only in emergency—when there is no other solution. Those marked ⊕ end with the third, which may be done occasionally; they violate no important rule. If the penultimate tone in the CF is the fifth, as in Ex. 20, there are many more possible endings.

USE OF TRIPLE METERS: 3/4, 3/2 AND 6/4

§ 35. If a measure is divided in three (3/4 and 3/2), it has only one accented beat. In 6/4, which is a combination of two 3/4s, there are two accented beats. If the quarter notes in 3/4 are divided into eighth notes, or the half notes of 3/2 into six quarter notes, the first of each pair of notes is relatively accented (see also § 15).

When one is writing in groups of three quarter notes—in 3/4—or in groups of three half notes—in 3/2—there can be consonances on all three beats, as in (*a*), or one dissonance on the third beat, as in (*b*), or one dissonance on the second beat, as in (*c*). If in 3/2 the half notes are divided into quarter notes, as in (*d*), the second, fourth, and sixth beats can be passing notes. Obviously the cambiata can be used in 3/2, but not in either 3/4 or 6/4 where a strong accented beat could not occur at both the beginning and ending of a cambiata. In the 6/4 examples among the following ones (see *e*), each of the three beats is treated like the three beats of 3/4.

cambiata ?

COMMENT ON EXAMPLES IN THIRD SPECIES, EXS. 19–26

These examples contain a number of errors or violations of rules. Ordinarily they are not too objectionable, some are even tolerable. They are included here for two reasons: (1) because many of them provide an opportunity for introducing an interval or succession of tones which could not have been applied otherwise. Thus in Ex. 19, ms. 6, for example, there are not many ways of introducing the fifth, *a*, below the *e* of the CF. 19*l* shows one possibility, and 19*m* might be changed in the following manner in ms. 5 to lead to this *a* also:

Ex. 19*m*

Similar cases are to be found elsewhere in these examples, but these do not justify other violations, some of which are intolerable. A few of these can be corrected, as the following shows:

(2) It seems useful to demonstrate such violations, so that the student will become watchful in similar situations. There is in 25*i*, for instance, a temptation to write open parallel 5s (at ⊗) because there is only one solution; this in itself violates a rule—that a leap should not be made in the same direction as a preceding melodic line—but that is a lesser failing in many cases. See also the intermittent 8s and primes in 19*e*, *l*, *q*, 20*h*, *i*, *l*, 22*a*, *k* (very bad), and 26*f* (tolerable). When there is no other solution, these may possibly be tolerated if four or more tones and an interval of a fourth lie between them. The same is true for intermittent 5s.

There is perhaps no excuse for such violations as the leaps made in 19*g* when an even better continuation is possible:

Neither can one excuse octave leaps up and down in one small segment, as in 20*h* and *i*.

In the penultimate measure one may occasionally use a melodic line containing two dissonances in succession like that in 25*a*, ms. 6. The scale line is a fair excuse for a slight violation of this kind.

In Exs. 22 and 23 the cambiata is used on almost every available beat. More than two cambiatas would have been possible in each added line, but in such a short melody two are more than enough.

The student is warned not to begin a cambiata on a weak beat, especially in 6/4 meter, as shown below:

The third beat, as in (*a*), and the fifth beat, as in (*b*), are weak beats. But starting a cambiata on one of the two strong beats would not help in this meter either, because it would then end on a weak beat (either the fifth or the second).

With quarter notes in 3/2, on the other hand, there are ample opportunities for cambiatas, since both beginning and ending are on strong beats.

Passing notes on strong beats are not always acceptable in 6/4. Those in 26k, ms. 3, might be tolerated, but the one in 26f almost gives the impression of belonging to a seventh-chord.

The student will find it useful to try correcting those errors or poor passages which are marked in the examples, and perhaps others too which he himself finds wrong.

In the Comment on Examples in Second Species (p. 25) the term 'sequential repetition' was used. The instance of this in Ex. 19b makes a more definite explanation of the term necessary.

In music the term *sequence* means primarily the repetition of a unit of any length when transposed to another degree. There are perfect, exact, partial, varied, developed, incomplete, semi- and quasi-sequences. In many cases only the melodic elements of the unit are repeated, that is, its intervals and its rhythmical and metrical features. If no change in any of these features occurs, except in so far as they are transposed, the sequence is *exact*. A *perfect* sequence will also repeat the harmony or the accompanying voices or the whole accompaniment. An *incomplete* sequence is one where some of the features are omitted. *Semi-* or *quasi*-sequences are sequences in which the harmony does not participate in the progression, for instance, or in which intervals and rhythms are changed. In *varied* sequences, embellishments will appear in the melody and/or accompaniment, and voices may be added, the vertical order of the voices changed (as in invertible counterpoint), and substitute tones and chromatics used in both melody and accompaniment, etc. *Developing* sequence may add to the latter changes of interval which tend towards a climax.

In addition, there is a distinction between *diatonic* sequences using only diatonic tones—and so disregarding the specific size of the intervals (major, minor, etc.)—and *chromatic* sequences using substitute tones for purposes of embellishment or for modulation.[1]

There is no employment of sequences in these preliminary exercises. On the contrary, they are deliberately avoided for two reasons. First, repetition is commonly used to emphasize a unit. It serves to impress the unit on the memory in anticipation of later use; and a beginner's technical resources would not be adequate to handle such problems. Secondly, there would not be enough space to fit in all that the use of sequences entails in the small compass of these short segments.

---

[1] For further discussion of sequences see *Structural Functions of Harmony*, Chapter XI.

Passing Notes

Ex. 20 (Note changes of clef in upper examples)

Ex. 21 Cambiata

Ex. 22 Cambiata

⊕ One may end occasionally with the 3rd.
▨ Fux in his *Gradus ad Parnassum* allows these forms: the forms marked ⊠, however, are better.

Ex. 24

Ex. 25

*) 2 dissonances tolerated in penultimate measure.

Ex. 26

IV

FOURTH SPECIES

*Syncopated half notes and suspensions in upper and lower voices added to the
cantus firmus*

ADVICE AND DIRECTIONS

§ 36. Syncopation occurs when an unaccented note is extended in duration by being
bound over to the next accented note:

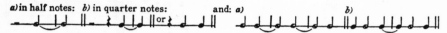

§ 37. In these preliminary studies the student should not use syncopations other than
those in which the note on the weak beat is at least as long as the tied note on the
strong beat:

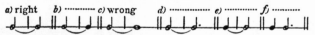

The last (*f*) is wrong because the dotted half note on the second beat, a weak beat,
is in fact a quarter note tied over to a longer half note on the strong third beat, thus:

§ 38.   In the fourth species only syncopated half notes will be used:

Both the half notes of which the syncopation consists may be consonant with the
notes of the CF:

But this, if continued for any length of time, is likely to become poor and stiff. There
is no strict interdict forbidding the interruption of tied half notes and their replacement by untied half notes for one or more measures. This combined with use of
passing notes contributes variety and freedom of movement.

THE THIRD CONVENTIONALIZED FORMULA: THE SUSPENSION

§ 39. Syncopation is used to the best advantage in the third conventionalized formula, the prepared and resolved dissonance, the *suspension*.

The suspension is a dissonance in a formula of three notes. The first note placed on a weak beat as a consonance with the CF, is the beginning of a syncopation and serves as the *preparation*. This note, held over, becomes a dissonance on the strong beat through the movement at that point of the CF. On the following weak beat the *resolution* is obtained by stepwise movement downward from the dissonance to a consonance with the CF (and with the other voices, if there are more than two). Thus the suspension, the dissonant note which is suspended from the preceding measure, is again a middle note between two consonances.

§ 40. The CF must never be considered a dissonance, a very frequent error on the part of beginners. Only the added voice can contain a dissonance. The suspension must never be led upward; it must always descend one step to the resolution.

§ 41. Every possible application of the suspension to each step of the CF should be examined systematically as was done with the passing note (Ex. 12) and the cambiata (Ex. 21). As can be seen in Ex. 27 where this is done, the dissonant intervals will resolve in the following manner:

In the upper voice:

The 7th resolves into a 6th,
The 4th resolves into a 3rd,
The 2nd resolves into a prime,
The 9th resolves into an 8ve,
The 11th resolves into a 10th.

In the lower voice:

The 2nd resolves into a 3rd,
The 4th resolves into a 5th,
The 9th resolves into a 10th,
The 11th resolves into a 12th.

42. BUT—and this rule must be strictly obeyed—the seventh must never be resolved into an octave. Accordingly *the seventh cannot be used as a suspension in the lower voice* (marked ⊓ in Ex. 27).

§ 43. Intermittent parallel 8s (marked ⊟ in Ex. 27) and intermittent parallel 5s (marked ⊗) are tantamount to open parallels. The suspension does not conceal this parallel movement. The suspension is only a postponement of the real movement and this dissonance in fact 'stands for its resolution'.

§ **44.** The cases marked X in Ex. 27 are not real suspensions because there is no dissonance. But in three or more voices they might become dissonances.

§ **45.** Beware of crossing of voices. See the cases marked 'crossing'.

§ **46.** There is no serious objection to a second resolving into a prime (marked ▱ in Ex. 27). This prime is neither better nor worse than any other prime. But one must admit that it obscures the voice leading (especially on the piano). The resolution of a ninth into an octave is perfectly correct as long as this octave does not produce emptiness, which happens sometimes.

§ **47.** Beginners often use a passing note as a syncopation and even as a preparation for a suspension. This is entirely wrong. The beginning of a syncopation, and especially that of a suspension, must be a consonance. Thus, all the following examples are incorrect:

COMMENT ON EXAMPLES IN FOURTH SPECIES, EXS. 28 AND 29

If the CF uses as penultimate tone the leading (7th) tone of the scale there are only two syncopations (both of them suspensions) possible in the upper voice, those of 4–3 (or 11–10)—as in 28c, d, m, n and p—and 7–6 (see 28e and q). Neither form would be usable in 28a because the one would demand the repetition of the tone e in ms. 7:

and the other would produce hidden 8s:

If there were not an *a* in ms. 7 of the CF, but a *g*, for example, instead, another syncopation leading to an ending on the third would be possible:

In the lower voice only one suspension is possible, 2–3, as in 28*h* and *s*, and one other syncopation as in 28*r*. Here also the above mentioned change in the CF would open the way for another syncopation:

To repeat, do not connect a suspension to a passing note as in 28*t*. This is a wrong preparation. But if a syncopation ends with a consonance, a passing note can follow (see 28*d*, ms. 6 or 29*b*, ms. 3). Note the intermittent 8s, primes, and 5s in 28*d*, *f*, *h* and *i* respectively.

Some of the examples are poor because they do not contain many syncopations, either consonant or dissonant. Some might be excused because a syncopation not used in a preceding example is introduced, e.g. the low *c* in 28*j* (ms. 3), or 29*l* (ms. 8), or 29*m* (ms. 3), or 29*p* (ms. 7). But it is doubtful whether this would justify interrupting the prescribed movement in syncopations. However, these are not compositions but only exercises to be done as well as possible.

Suspensions

Ex. 27

☐ Intermittent 8s between preparation and resolution forbidden.
⊗   ,,   5s   ,,   ,,   ,,   ,,   ,,
☐ 7 resolving to 8 in lower voice forbidden.
◫ 9-8 and 2-1 in upper voice permitted.
✕ 6-5 or 5-6 not real suspensions.
⊞ Resolution correct if perfect 5, not dim. 5.
⊕ Possible as a passing note.

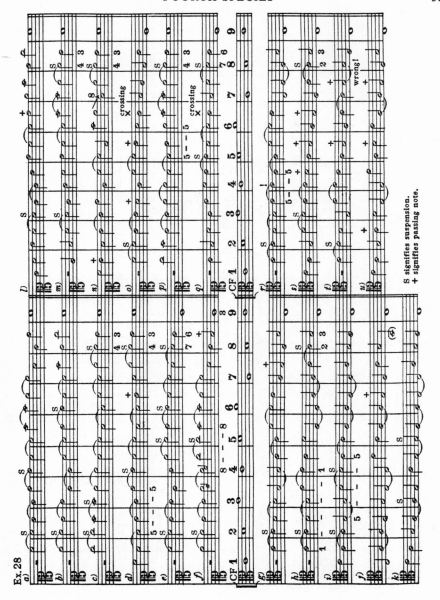

S signifies suspension.
+ signifies passing note.

Ex. 29

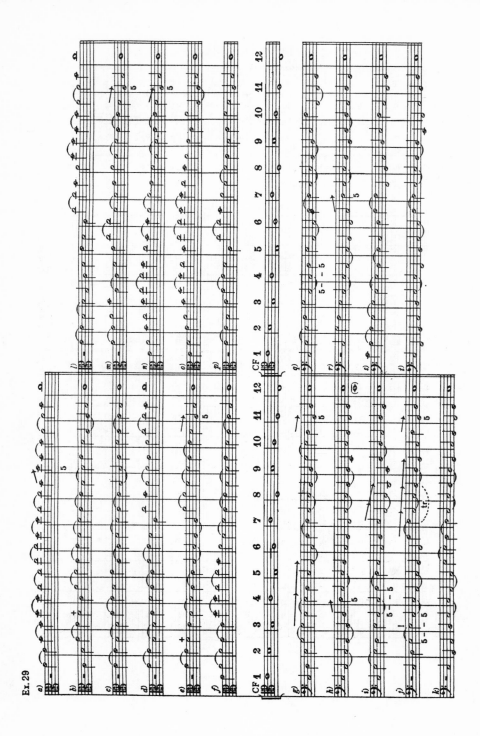

V

FIFTH SPECIES

Mixed notes added to the cantus firmus

ADVICE AND DIRECTIONS: RHYTHMS

§ **48.** Notes of various lengths are to be used in lower and upper voices: whole notes, half notes, quarter notes, and, occasionally, even eighth notes; syncopations of half notes, and sometimes of quarter notes (see (*a*) below); dotted half notes on the first beat (*b*) or, as at (*c*), tied from the second beat; dotted quarter notes (*d*); rhythms like (*e*) and (*f*); and groups of eighth notes (*g*)—all of these may be used:

§ **49.** Some restrictions concerning the use of syncopations have been discussed in § 37. They are, of course, binding here as well. There are a number of other rhythmical restrictions.

§ **50.** Rhythms of this kind: [musical example] should be avoided as far as possible or used only under certain conditions. The old rule which forbade these rhythms perhaps had its origin in the tendency of sacred music to avoid the vulgarity of 'dancelike' rhythms. This rule allowed subdivision of the first half note of a 2/4 or 3/4 measure only if (1) the next half note or half notes were subdivided: [musical example] or (2) the first small note was tied over from a half note of the preceding measure and a new syncopation followed:

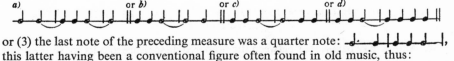

or (3) the last note of the preceding measure was a quarter note: [musical example], this latter having been a conventional figure often found in old music, thus:

The cambiata often appears in this form:

§ **51.** Eighth notes should not be used too frequently and there should seldom be more than two of them in a measure; as a rule they should come on the second or fourth beats:

§ **52.** All smaller notes, that is eighth notes and even quarter notes, too, are best used towards the end of an example. Introducing them near the beginning often causes imbalance because of the tendency of the smallest notes to increase in number. Once they are brought in, this *tendency of the smallest notes* may cause them to over-run an entire example. It is very difficult on the one hand for a beginner to neutralize this tendency, and, on the other, usage of smaller notes towards the end produces a climaxing effect which would be lost if this possibility had been exhausted in the preceding measures. Accordingly it is better to begin with long notes, not using even quarter notes too early, and to use eighth notes only sparingly near the end.

§ **53.** Some of these rhythms are combined below with other rhythms in two voices, for example, the dotted half note (at ⊞), the quarter rest at the beginning (at ⊗), a half note and two quarter notes (at ⊕), etc.

THE FOURTH CONVENTIONALIZED FORMULA: THE INTERRUPTED RESOLUTION

§ **54.** A note may be inserted between the prepared dissonance and its resolution; this note should usually be consonant with the CF. The suspended note is thus reduced to a quarter note on the strong beat, the interrupting consonance standing on the next weak beat and the resolution on the third beat.

§ **55.** Usually the interrupting note is a second, third or fourth lower than the suspension. In no case should a leap larger than a fifth be used.

Forms like those under (*a*) in the foregoing example, will thus come to look like those under (*b*). The interruption may sometimes consist of two eighth notes, as at (*c*). The resolution then occurs at the first eighth note. The second eighth note will be either consonant or an auxiliary note (as at *) one step below the resolution that returns at the third beat to the consonant resolution.

At ① a leap of a fifth is preferable to the tritone as the note of interruption, but at ⊠ a tritone is the only usable note; this is perhaps the first case in which it may be tolerated—because it is unavoidable.

§ **56.** There occur examples where it is not possible to use a lower note as interruption. In such cases it is customary to use an upper note (see (*a*) below). Occasionally an upper note is actually to be preferred, as at (*b*) where the note *a* provides a better interruption than *e*.

§ **57.** Since the suspension does not correct intermittent parallel 8s or 5s, clearly the interrupted resolution will not either. In two voices in particular they are too noticeable.

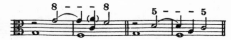

COMMENT ON EXAMPLES IN FIFTH SPECIES, EXS. 30 AND 31

Reasons for avoiding sequences in the following exercises were given under Comment on Examples in Third Species (pp. 36 ff.), but there are also other sorts of repetition which are not usable here. In 30*i*, mss. 2, 4 and 6, there appears a syncopated half note (at X). Through such repetition a feeling of subdivision into four 'phrases' (marked a, a′, a″) is produced. This should be avoided for reasons similar to those for excluding sequences. Besides, such phrasing comes a little too close to the style of popular songs and dances, the construction of which is based on principles differing fundamentally from those of contrapuntal exercises.

In § 52 the tendency of the smallest notes was discussed. 30*d* and 30*j* (at ▱) are good illustrations of the lameness of a melody whose movement is suddenly stopped by longer notes coming after many smaller notes.

The monotony produced by the repetition of the highest tone in a melody can be observed in 30*k* and 31*a*. Such a tone may assume the effect of a climax (for example, in an ascending line) and is better preserved for that effect.

See also the wrong cambiata beginning on a weak beat in 30*l*, mss. 6–7.

In 30*h* only an upper tone is available if an interruption is to be used in ms. 5.

The CF in Ex. 31 lies too high and forces the alto to rise several times to the treble *d–e–f*. In such a case the student had better transpose the CF.

Ex. 30

VI

THE MINOR TONALITY

DERIVATION OF MINOR[1]

§ 58. The minor tonality is treated here in a way similar to that in which the modes are treated, especially the Aeolian mode.[2]

§ 59. There are seven modes; each of them begins and ends with a tone of the diatonic scale and uses these diatonic tones in their basic unaltered form:

Thus each tone of the diatonic scale is treated as the tonic of a scale. The scale beginning with the 7th tone was never used very much apparently and fell into disuse long ago. Even its name is uncertain: it will not be discussed here.

All these scales can be transposed to other keys; they would begin at the equivalent

[1] The treatment of minor was suggested to this author by the theory of Simon Sechter, the renowned Viennese theorist.

[2] The present discussion of the modes does not aim at teaching the style of ancient composers; it aims exclusively at producing a bridge between strict counterpoint and the richer harmony of the composers of the eighteenth and nineteenth centuries.

This writer believes that no contemporary composer need be able to write in modal style. Doing this can only be compared to using candle light when one has electric light. It was understandable, of course, for those 'grandees' whose castles and palaces contained artistically elaborated walls, or even murals or frescoes, to refuse to destroy these works of art by installing electric wires. A peculiar result of such conservatism was that the old Emperor Franz Josef of Austria had no telephone in his summer castle at Schoenbrunn and could only communicate with his ministers by means of a courier riding on horseback.

In music we do not have to defend valuable murals. Accordingly, we need not return to older forms of musical life, but can enjoy the benefits of progress. This writer believes that the ancient modes—Greek or Medieval—are more perfect attempts at tonality than the pentatonic or the exotic scales, but that they are steps only towards the diatonic major scales (for more on this subject see *Harmonielehre*). The modes, then, would not be brought in here at all, were it not that they offer some advantages in the writing of fugues, as will be seen later. It is only because of this—and only in so far as there are any advantages—that these scales are discussed here; the aim is not the achievement of a 'modal style'. (*Editor's note*: the above discussion of the modes was derived from another statement by the author, not originally included in this book.)

tones in the scale and use the tones of these keys as their material. Thus, transposed to Eb, A or D, for instance, Dorian would still begin with the 2nd, Aeolian with the 6th, and Phrygian with the 3rd tone of the keys.

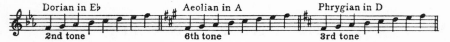

Three of the six modes are major-like because their tonic is a major triad:

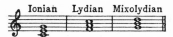

Three are minor-like:

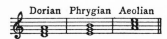

The Ionian scale, identical with our major scale, is undeniably the true natural product of the physical conditions of the tone, because it is based on the relations between the three main triads, which also contain the seven tones of the diatonic scale:

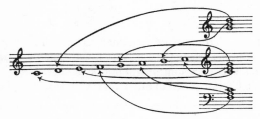

In comparison, the other modes are imperfect and primitive attempts at an interpretation of the secrets of nature. And they represent an imperfect and primitive organization of melody and harmony. The shortcomings of this organization are most evident in the unsatisfactory position of the half-steps, in particular in the absence of a leading tone (7th to 8th tone) in four of them.

Probably in consequence of these shortcomings, a process began which made the modes obsolete and finally caused progressive composers of the seventeenth century to abandon them entirely. This process is to be observed principally in a tendency of the major-like Lydian and Mixolydian modes to become similar to the Ionian mode, and of the minor-like Dorian, and to some extent the Phrygian, to resemble the Aeolian mode. But there also took place a mutual *rapprochement* between the major-like and the minor-like modes as well, the result of which was that major could contain almost every harmony of minor and vice versa.

§ **60.** The minor tonality is in its descending form, identical with the Aeolian mode. To procure a leading tone in the ascending scale in this mode, and then in the minor tonality also, the natural 7th tone was replaced by a tone a half-step lower than the 8th tone:

§ **61.** This replacement produced an interval of an augmented second between the natural 6th and the 'substitute' 7th tone. All augmented and diminished intervals were strictly forbidden by the composers of strict counterpoint. So to avoid this forbidden interval the 6th tone also was replaced by a substitute tone a half-step higher than the natural 6th tone:

§ **62.** The cadential effect of these substitute tones is necessary for a definite ending, but they also appear frequently in non-cadential segments.

§ **63.** The ending of the descending scale is the same as that of the major scale: 2 to 1, a whole step. Accordingly the descending scale needs no substitutes:

THE FOUR TURNING-POINTS AND THE PROCESS OF NEUTRALIZATION

§ **64.** The treatment of the minor scale will be regulated thus: the 7th and 6th tones will be considered as *turning-points*, that is, as points where the melody turns either upward towards the 8th tone, or downward away from it.

§ **65.** There are four turning-points:

The first: the substitute 7th tone:

It was introduced for the exclusive purpose of providing a leading tone to the 8th tone. Accordingly, if used, no tone may follow it but the 8th tone.

The second: the substitute 6th tone:

It was introduced for the exclusive purpose of avoiding the augmented interval produced by the substitute 7th tone. It would not be used if no substitute tone were to follow. Accordingly, if it is used, no tone but the substitute 7th tone can follow.

§ **66.** Evidently, if these rules are to be kept, chromatic progressions, like the following, must be strictly forbidden:

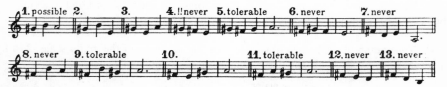

§ **67.** The following progressions are excluded also, although some of them, marked 'possible' and 'tolerable', might be usable later when the student has become conscious of the danger they offer to well-balanced harmony:

The reason for this strict and absolute interdict is simply a pedagogical one: it is to protect the student from making mistakes which could not be remedied without a great number of rules and exceptions. It is evident that many of the forms excluded thereby are commonplace in music of almost every period.[1]

§ **68.** The remaining two turning-points can be treated a little less strictly in some respects. There appear in minor segments in which none but the natural tones (of the descending scale) are used. These segments are less characteristic of minor and

---

[1] (*Editor's note*: the following statement of the author's, derived from another source, is also pertinent to this discussion.)

Advice which helps a beginner to solve simple problems in a manner not too foreign to a musician's feelings is subject to change. As an illustration there may be used the treatment of minor taught in this treatise. The obligation of the turning points and of neutralization does not even correspond to the technique of the modes, and less to that of Bach. But in the early stages, though it makes many things more difficult, it also helps to avoid severe faults. But soon after these preliminary studies, advice will be given on how to write more freely in minor, because one can assume that the student's sense of form, melody, and harmony will be developed by then and that he will be able to find out by ear what is wrong and how to correct it.

even resemble relative major. Accordingly, the rules for the third and fourth turning-points can be formulated so as to govern those instances in which the segment begins to turn towards the characteristic features of minor, i.e. where the substitute tones are to be brought in.

Third turning-point: the 7th tone in the descending scale must be 'resolved' or 'neutralized' by descending to the 6th natural tone, if and before any of the voices turns to the use of a substitute 7th tone:

Fourth turning-point: the 6th natural tone must be 'resolved' or 'neutralized' by descending to the 5th tone of the scale, if and before any of the voices turns to the use of a substitute 6th tone:

§ **69.** The *neutralization* of the natural 7th and 6th tones need not be accomplished at once, or every time one of these tones appears. It may be postponed until the need arises, i.e. when a substitute tone is to appear.

§ **70.** Accordingly, such progressions as the following are interdicted and should be corrected—in the manner shown in the lower system of the next example, for instance:

§ **71.** If substitute tones appear in 'cross relation' with natural tones, neutralization of every voice involved must be accomplished if and before a cross-related 6th or 7th tone is used in any one of the voices.[1]

---

[1] It should be mentioned that not only did the old theorists allow progressions like the following ones,

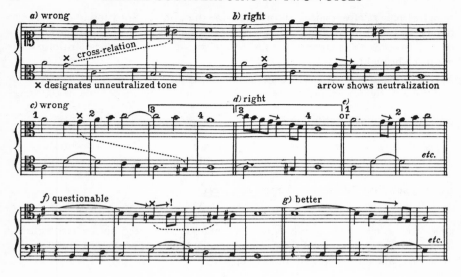

COMMENT ON EXAMPLES IN MINOR, EXS. 32–39

The need for *neutralization*—its fulfilment is marked 'neutr. - - -' in many of the examples—often forces one to lead the voices into some undesirable registers. See, for example, the low tones in 32*f* and *j*, and 35*j*. In the first and second species especially, fluency in the melody is much obstructed by the avoidance of cross relations. Thus, for example, in 32*d*, *g*, and *h* neither the natural 6th tone, *a♭* (marked *), nor the substitute 6th tone (marked □) can be used in ms. 6. The natural 7th tone, *b♭* (marked ▥), is impossible in 32*i*, ms. 4. In 33*a*, if *f* appears in ms. 3 there is no possibility of neutralization. In 33*b*, neutralization only becomes possible if syncopation is used. In 34*f*, the bass is forced down to low *d* in ms. 7, in 34*g*, ms. 3, the low *f* (at ✗) should not remain unneutralized. In 35*f* and *i*, at ⧄, the neutralization of the natural 6th tone, *f*, is unnecessary because no substitute 6th tone, *f♯*, follows.

but the old composers actually used them, too—to us these idioms appear rather more stylistic than essential; therefore they are not to be recommended for use:

The ending often presents difficulties. The lower voices in 32*g*, *h*, and *i* (and the upper voice in 32*d*, too) can only end in 8s with the CF—but they may do this if contrary motion is possible, as at X. Some of the upper voices in Ex. 32 use *d* to the *g* of the CF in the penultimate measure (at +), which is correct as a 2–1 ending.

In 34*f*, ms. 10, the g♯ does not go directly to *a*. This could be tolerated in the penultimate measure; it could be regarded as an interrupted resolution. A license might be permitted in the penultimate measures of 36*d*, *i* and *j*, also: but two consecutive dissonances would not be allowed in other places even if they were passing ones. Another license is permitted in 37*b* and *d* for the ending. The dissonant *c* on a strong beat in 38*e*, ms. 2, would be inadmissible if it were not the only way of justifying the b♭ in ms. 3. Observe also the dissonant *g* on the strong beat of 38*h*, ms. 3.

There are two places where it seemed difficult to continue correctly at all: 34*d*, ms. 9, and 35*b*, ms. 5. In the latter case one is faced with the difficulty of avoiding parallel 5s. One could use a quarter note on the first beat in ms. 5, but this would not avoid the intermittent parallel 5s, and it would not produce 'mixed notes'.

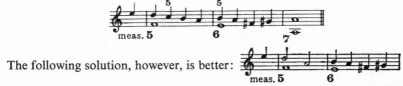

The following solution, however, is better:

The cambiata in ms. 10 of 34*d* is allowed by Fux. One might tolerate it in the penultimate measure if there were no better solution, though not in the middle of an example; however, one should never do so without a special reason. The octave *b* to the CF can only be approached in contrary motion. Admitting 'exceptionally' two consecutive dissonances, as in (*a*) and (*d*) of the following example (ms. 9), makes this

D

possible. But the solution in (*b*) and (*c*), ending on the third in ms. 11, should be preferred.

In 34*g*, ms. 4, the last tone *f* (at *) crosses the tenor. This was forbidden in previous exercises. It must still be excluded for the time being except in cases of emergency (i.e. when no other solution is possible) or when there is an especially good reason for it, as here: the tone *g* in ms. 5 could only be introduced by using this crossing or the following one:

As crossing is not in fact wrong, but forbidden here only for pedagogical reasons, one might once in a while forget pedagogy.

Minor: First Species

Ex. 32

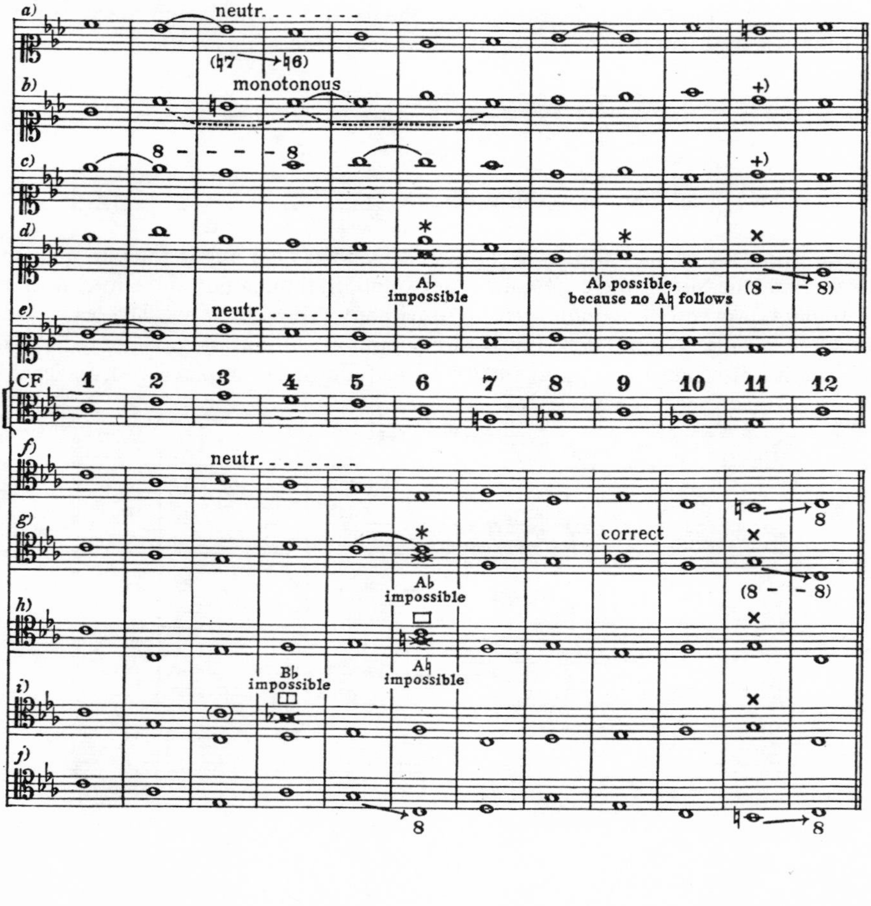

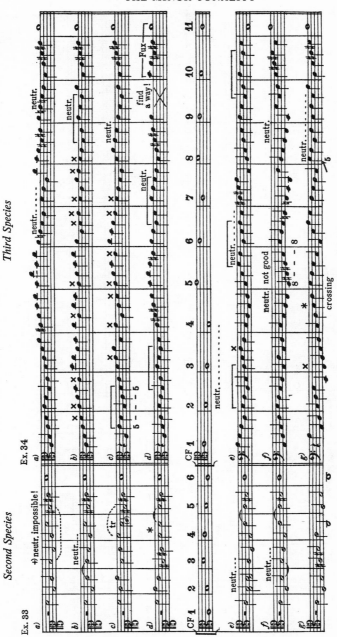

x signifies tones which are to be neutralized.

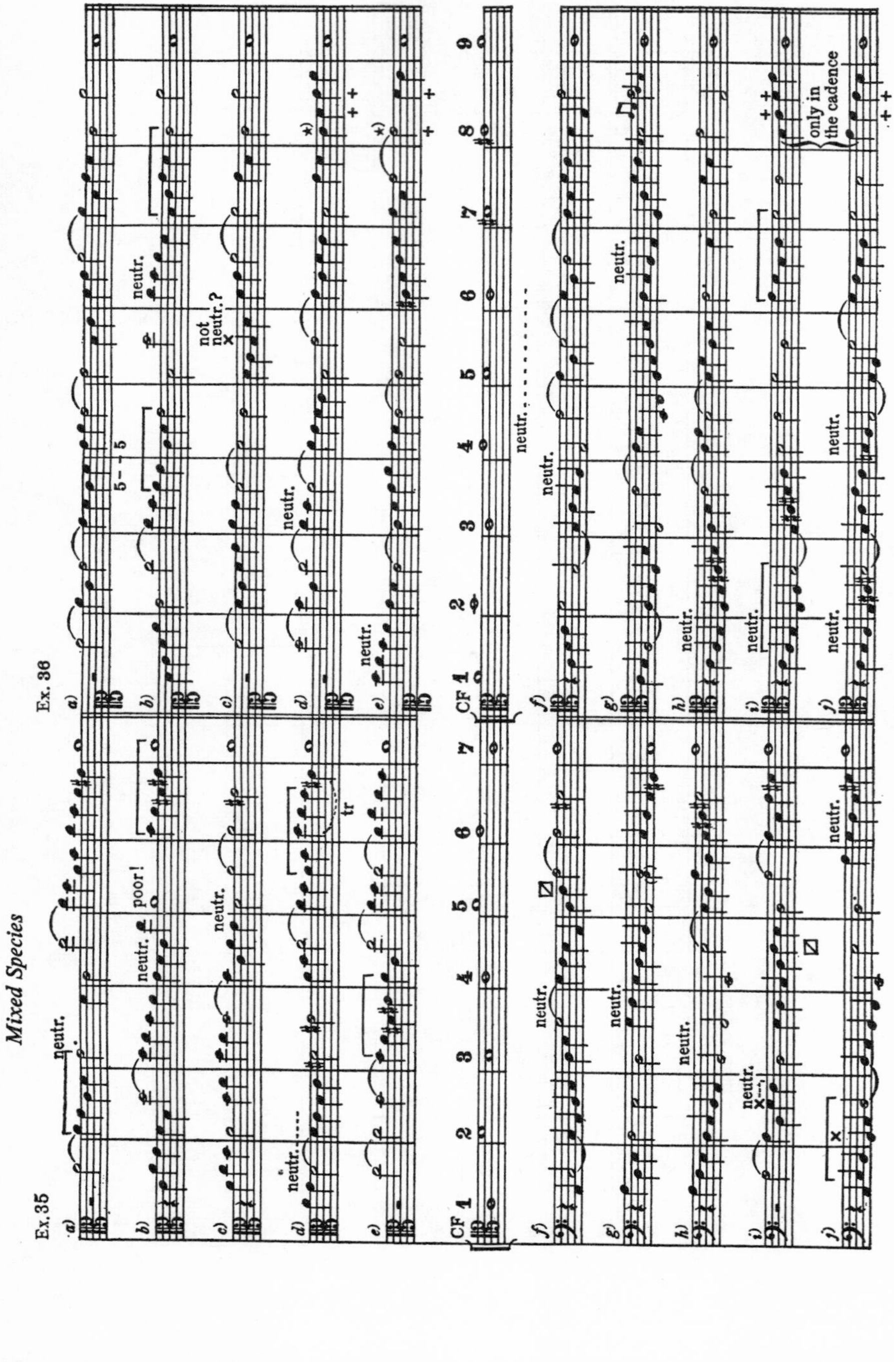

*) admissible only in cadence.

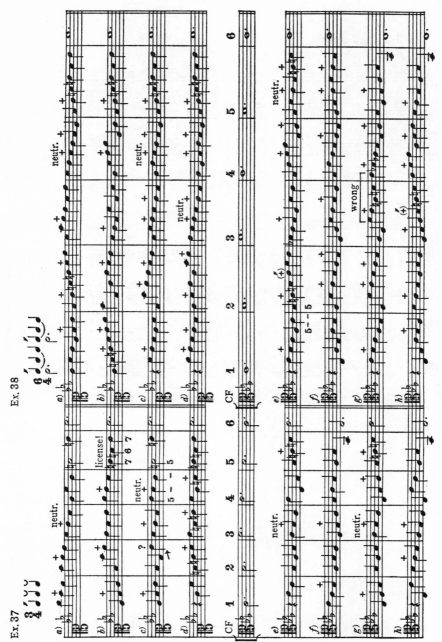

Ex. 39

VII

FIRST COMPOSITIONAL APPLICATION:
CADENCES WITHOUT *CANTUS FIRMUS*

CADENCES AND THE EXPRESSION OF TONALITY

§ **72.** The principles for building cadences in counterpoint are the same as those the student knows from his studies in harmony. The tonality must be expressed incontestably in either case.

§ **73.** For this reason those characteristics of a tonality must be introduced which distinguish it most clearly from other tonalities and above all from those to which it has the greatest similarity.

§ **74.** Scales which differ by only *one* tone have the greatest number of common tones, and thus resemble each other in the highest degree. The tone or tones by which a tonality is distinguishable from other tonalities can be called its 'characteristic(s)'. Their presence increases, and their absence decreases, the functional distinction of a single voice or combination of several voices, and of a short segment or longer piece of music.

§ **75.** Clearly, of the following melodies (*a*) could represent *C* major as well as *G* major, (*b*) *C* major or *F* major, (*c*) *C* major or *G* major, or even *F* major.

§ **76.** Even two voices might become indefinite if they abstained from producing the characteristics of a tonality. The following segment, for example, can be understood in at least two ways. In (*a*) the added bass by using *f*♮ decides in favour of *C* major; in (*b*) the *f*♯ suggests *G* major.

*) The monotony in *b*) is due to the fact that the *f*♯ could only appear in the added bass voice and had to appear there several times.

But that one of the foregoing melodies (§ 75*c*) can really imply at least three keys is proven by the four different treatments in the next example. In (*a*) this little segment is in the soprano, in (*b*) it is in the alto, in (*c*) it is in the tenor, and in (*d*) it appears in the bass (the second half of ms. 4 is changed and an extra measure added so that the bass can end on *f*).

§ **77.** The demonstration of the tonal vagueness of the preceding examples discloses that, apart from the tonic at the beginning and the end, the characteristics of a major tonality are the 4th and 7th tones.

§ **78.** The 4th tone represents the subdominant region (IV and II), and thus prevents the interpretation of a segment as expressing a tonality a fifth above.

§ **79.** The 7th tone represents the dominant region (V), and thus prevents the interpretation of a segment as expressing a tonality a fifth below.

§ **80.** To achieve a cadential effect these two tones, or their substitutes, must appear immediately before the final tonic. But they must also be present in the parts preceding the ending or else the ending may be vague.

§ **81.** In an authentic cadence[1] these characteristic tones will appear in the same order as taught in harmony: i.e. elements of IV (or II), followed by those of V and then I.

§ **82.** In two-voice counterpoint the production of full triads is not feasible. But the co-operation of the two voices may be such that every doubt is excluded. There may be, at one point, in one voice, or both, a characteristic part of a scale line (or tones from it), which in itself is sufficient to express a key; see, for instance, ms. 6 of 40*a*: it contains all the tones of *C* major as well as expressing IV on the first, second and third beats, and V on the fourth beat. At another, one of the voices (see the tenor in 40*e*, ms. 6) may contribute the fifth and the root of V while the other voice (see the alto) sustains the third. Of course, some cadential formulas such as that in the bass in 40*d*, ms. 5 (which is in addition preceded by an entire scale), are in themselves definite enough to suggest an ending. See also the tenor in 40*e*.

§ **83.** The melodic progressions which lead distinctly to the tonic in this way are given below. Many are more suitable as upper voices, and some are more suitable as lower voices. But a great number are usable in both ways. All of these progressions may be employed by the student in his cadences.

Major
a) Upper Voice

b) Lower Voice

---

[1] The plagal cadence is of no concern here; it does not teach the student anything of technical importance, though in a composition it might produce a stylistic effect.

HOW TO PROCEED WITHOUT A GIVEN *CANTUS FIRMUS*

§ 84. In § 52 the *tendency of the smallest notes* was discussed and the student was advised to begin with longer notes, and postpone smaller notes. One of the voices had best begin with a longer note, while the other uses smaller ones. The voice using the longer notes may then be treated like a CF.

§ 85. Syncopations are very useful, especially if they prepare a suspension. As the suspension must be resolved on the next beat, a continuation is provided.

§ 86. By means of the preceding exercises the student should be able to remember a certain number of melodic progressions and their relation and applicability to a second voice. Such progressions will help him to find continuations. Also helpful are other conventionalized formulas, such as the cambiata and the interrupted resolution.

§ **87.** Now more than ever the student must 'listen' to his voices as regards their fluency. A melody will often reveal a tendency to move in a certain direction. And often a change of register must take place for the avoidance of monotony. This latter is frequently caused by repetition of tones or successions of tones, and also by voices remaining too long in one register or moving too much in one direction.

§ **88.** An example of how to proceed without a CF now follows:

Suppose that the soprano begins with a whole note tied over to the second measure: This note can be treated in many ways. It can remain a consonance, as in the following examples, although a consonance does not usually produce a good beginning for a continuation:

A dissonance, i.e. a suspension, will produce a better continuation, an advantage the beginner should remember when he has to work without a given voice and is not yet in a position to use motifs.

In the following example the movement of the second voice can make this tied note a seventh (as at (*a*) and (*d*)), a fourth ((*b*) and (*c*)), a second ((*e*)), or a ninth ((*f*)). The latter two intervals, however, are scarcely usable here.

The lower voice might also move in the following ways if the upper voice is suspended:

Or, if the lower voice is suspended, the upper voice might move like this:

However, the following two suspensions are impossible for well-known reasons:

After such beginnings one may continue by always treating the longest note like a CF against which there can be written either notes of the same length (as in first species) or smaller notes (as in the other species). However, one should not use the suspension too regularly—in the upper voice one measure and in the lower the next, etc. The most effective procedure is best decided upon by 'listening' to the tendency of each of the voices and continuing them freely according to this tendency. Especially to be avoided is the definite production of regular 'phrasing'.

The examples need not be more than five to seven measures long, but less than four measures is too short. As soon as one has written three or four measures one should begin preparing for a conclusion, using progressions like those in § 83 for this.

The student should try concluding the following examples:

§ 89. The following treatments of the suspension are of considerable use: the second voice might move (1) simultaneously with the suspension into another consonant resolution (as at X in (c) of the preceding and (a) of the following example), or (2) during the course of the suspension by step or leap before the resolution occurs with a consonance (as happens in nearly all of the following examples). A consonant tone is preferable for leaps, while in stepwise movement both consonances and dissonances may appear.

In (*e*) a ninth (marked ⊠ in this and other examples) is produced by contrary motion, and the voice then proceeds stepwise through a consonance to meet the resolution. But in (*f*) the ninth enters in an alarming manner, causing suspicion. In anticipation of the upper voice becoming a suspension, the ninth is introduced in a motion parallel with that of the resolution, making one suspect parallel 8s. But parallel 8s never in fact occur because when the resolution takes place the lower voice has eluded the danger by contrary motion. This could also be achieved by means of a cambiata:

In (*i*) a similar problem concerning the ninth is solved by continuing the descent step-wise so that a third is made with the resolution.

Leaps to tones consonant with the suspension can be seen in (*m*), (*o*), (*p*), (*q*) and (*r*) (at ⊗). Tones dissonant to the suspension, as in (*k*), (*l*) and (*n*) (at ⊡), are used on the grounds that they would be consonant with the resolution, although they make the suspension twice a dissonance—7 and 4 in (*k*), 4 and 7 in (*l*) and 4 and 2 in (*n*).

COMMENT ON CADENCES, EXAMPLE 40

These examples are longer than necessary, especially those in minor. Some might have been made shorter if, after neutralization in one voice, the other voice had not entered into a situation requiring neutralization, too. Thus, 40g could have ended after ms. 4 in this manner:

But as it is, practice in fluent writing, and particularly in writing in minor, helps to overcome the difficulties raised by the turning-points. The student should not mind writing long examples if he can, at the same time, avoid monotony.

Observe the alto in ms. 3 of 40i. It makes the tenor a dissonance on the first beat, but in turn becomes a suspension itself, a suspension correctly prepared—it begins as a consonance on a weak beat (second)—and resolved on the fourth beat. The only differences between this and previous procedures are that the size of the notes has been halved—there are quarter notes where there were half notes formerly—and that what only came on the first strong beat formerly, occurs here on the second strong beat.

Cadences

Ex. 40 (cont.)

VIII

SECOND COMPOSITIONAL APPLICATION: CADENCES TO VARIOUS REGIONS; MODULATION

REGIONS AND MODULATION

§ **90.** For reasons of form contrast is necessary, even in smaller compositions. Among the most effective ways of obtaining it are functional changes in the structure of the harmony.

§ **91.** In former times, if, in a piece or a segment of it, there appeared one or more tones foreign to the tonality, if in particular such a segment moved with the use of cadential features to a degree other than the tonic, one used to speak of a *modulation*. This may have been correct in the earlier stages of music when a foreign tone amongst mere tonal harmonies was really an outstanding event. But in Bach's time, and even before, this term modulation was no longer adequate.

§ **92.** The term modulation is only adequate if (*a*) a tonality has been abandoned definitely and for a considerable time, and (*b*) another tonality has been established. For this reason one should speak more often of a change from one *region* of a tonality to another *region* of the same tonality, than of a modulation. In this treatise, however, the term modulation will often be used to describe the change from one region to another.[1]

THE RELATIONSHIP OF REGIONS

§ **93.** The closest relatives of a major tonality are its relative minor (submediant), the dominant and its relative minor (mediant), and the subdominant and its relative minor

---

[1] I have introduced the term *region* in order to establish and strengthen the principle of *monotonality*, which aims at a unified apprehension of the harmonic movement within a piece of music. By means of this concept the distinction between enriched or extended tonality and modulation will be sharpened. If, as stated above, tones and progressions of harmonies appear in a piece or some of its segments, which are not diatonic, this need not be considered a modulation. If the movement establishes one of the degrees as a tonic with the aid of cadential features, this might be considered a change of region. If the movement fails to settle down, this should be considered as a case of *roving* harmony. For more on this subject see *Structural Functions of Harmony*, where all of the regions are evaluated. Movement or modulation to remote regions is not included in these preliminary contrapuntal exercises. Accordingly, the list of available regions given in § 93 is reduced so as to include only those which will be used in these exercises.

(dorian). In the following chart these relationships and also those of the minor tonality are explained:

THE CLOSEST RELATIVES OF MAJOR

*Regions**   *Degrees*   *In C Major*

THE CLOSEST RELATIVES OF MINOR

*Regions**   *Degrees*   *In A Minor*

*List of Abbreviations:

(Capital letters indicate major-like regions.
Small letters indicate minor-like regions.)

T and *t* indicate tonic.   *SM* and *sm* indicate submediant.
D indicates dominant.   *M* and *m* indicate mediant.
v indicates five-minor.   *dor* indicates dorian.
SD and *sd* indicate subdominant.   *subT* indicates subtonic.[1]

§ 94. These relationships express approximately the relationships between the modes. Note that as VII in major and II in minor are diminished triads no regions are based upon them.

§ 95. Modulations to each of these regions are carried out in the examples mentioned below:

From a major tonality there is
   modulation to the region of

   (1) Submediant (relative minor), in
      Ex. 41.

From a minor tonality there is
   modulation to the region of

   (1) Mediant (relative major), in
      Ex. 42.

---

[1] This region, which is called the subtonic in *Structural Functions of Harmony*, may seem remote if one does not take into account the fact that Aeolian is only a 'mode' of major. In general, therefore, minor has the same relatives as major.

From a major tonality there is
modulation to the region of

(2) Dominant, in Ex. 44.
(3) Mediant, in Ex. 45.
(4) Subdominant, in Ex. 46.
(5) Dorian, in Ex. 47.

From a minor tonality there is
modulation to the region of

(2) Five-minor, in Ex. 48.
(3) Subtonic, in Ex. 49.
(4) Subdominant, in Ex. 50.
(5) Submediant, in Ex. 51.

MODULATIONS TO RELATED REGIONS

§ **96.** These shall be carried out in short sentences, six to ten measures in length, in accordance with the following directions:

Every change of region requires neutralization of the cross-related tones and the employment of melodic lines that are neutral, that is, melodic lines which contain a number of tones common to the two regions concerned. The sentences shall therefore consist of four parts as follows:

(1) A statement of the tonality of departure. In simple cases the presentation of the tonic may be sufficient, but it is usually better to elaborate a little more.

(2) A neutral zone where only those tones appear which are common to both the regions and where the cross-related tones are neutralized, as in the procedure for minor (see §§ 64 ff.).

(3) The modulation proper, that is, the turning towards such tones as are characteristic of the tonality of the goal.

(4) Finally, a cadence in the tonality of the goal.

§ **97.** Comparison of the scales of the various regions as illustrated below will show which tones are cross-related (marked X), i.e. which have to be neutralized or can perform the modulation.

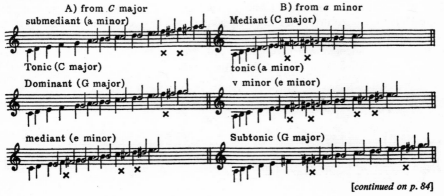

[continued on p. 84]

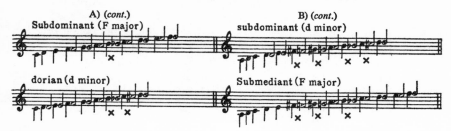

MAJOR TO RELATIVE MINOR (*sm*) AND MINOR TO RELATIVE MAJOR (*M*)

§ 98. In the descending major scale there are segments in which the 7th and 6th tones of the relative minor are neutralized because the descending minor scale is identical with the corresponding part of the major scale. This identity can be used for the change from major to relative minor (*sm*) and vice versa (*M*). This would account for a turn towards major in many of the examples given previously in minor (Exs. 32–35).

§ 99. In a similar manner examples in major can turn towards minor (*sm*), if and after every 5th tone (such as *g* in *C* major) has been neutralized downward into a 4th tone (*f*), and every 4th tone into a 3rd tone (*e*), as if they were 7th and 6th tones of relative minor respectively. This procedure is illustrated in Ex. 41.

COMMENT ON MODULATIONS BETWEEN RELATIVE MAJOR AND MINOR REGIONS, EXS. 41 AND 42

All of these examples were previously cadences in major in Ex. 40. In each of them a point has been found where the aforementioned change of concept can be applied. In 41*a* neutralization of the *g* in the alto (ms. 3) precedes the application of substitutes in ms. 5, as it must. For this reason the initial *g* in the soprano had better be omitted. In 41*b*, ms. 4, one can tolerate the neutralization by means of an interrupted resolution. Here no substitute for the 6th tone is used. 41*c* has been changed slightly from the original in ms. 4.

In Ex. 42, cadences which originally appeared in minor (40*g* and *j*) now turn towards the relative major. This process starts taking place in ms. 5 of 42*a* and ms. 3 of 42*b*.

Ex. 41 from Major to Minor *(sm)*
a) (from 40*a*)

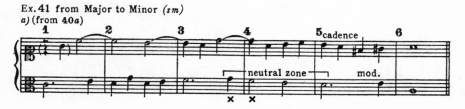

Ex. 42 from Minor to Major (*M*)

MODULATIONS WITH A GIVEN VOICE

§ **100.** It might be easier for the student to carry out these modulations to a CF or to a given voice in mixed notes at first. A few such voices are presented in the following examples. The words 'neutralization', 'modulation' and 'cadence' indicate approximately where these procedures may be applied. Both upper and lower voices are to be added.

from Major to Minor (*sm*)

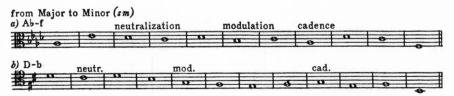

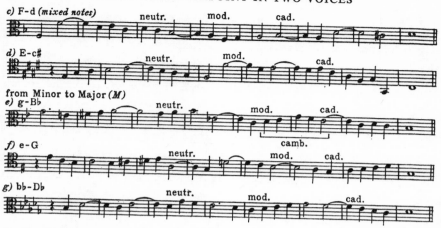

In Ex. 43 four of these exercises are worked out.

COMMENT ON MODULATIONS WITH GIVEN VOICES, EXAMPLE 43

In 43*a*, the neutralization in the alto voice occurs in ms. 3. The great distance between these two voices is a minor shortcoming. In 43*b*, ms. 5, the resolution of the suspension *d* into *c* coincides with an *f♯*; this can be excused since the latter can be considered as part of a cambiata. Compare 42*a*, ms. 3, where the cambiata does not end on a consonance because the *f♯* in the alto is a suspension which resolves on the second beat. This may be tolerated too.

The cadence in 43*b* is a little weak because the subdominant is not expressed distinctly enough, at least in the bass. Besides, the intermittent parallel 5s in mss. 3 and 4 are objectionable. The same is also true of 43*c*, mss. 1 and 2, although this example has a better cadence.

In 43*d*, the same given voice has been used as in 43*c*, but here an upper voice—the soprano—has been added. This voice is rather fluent but the cadence is again a little indefinite.

MODULATIONS TO OTHER REGIONS

§ **101.** Modulations or cadences which connect the closely related regions indicated on the chart can be produced in much the same way as modulations from major to relative minor (Ex. 40). Such modulations, too, can be executed with the characteristic tones of the tonality of the goal, after neutralization. Note that all of the examples below have rather long cadences to enable the voices to bring in the tones peculiar to the new regions.

COMMENT ON MODULATIONS TO OTHER REGIONS, EXS. 44–51

In a modulation to the *dominant* region the 4th tone of the tonality of departure (*f* in C major) is cross-related with the dominant's leading tone (*f♯*). In 44*a*, ms. 2, the descending progression eliminates the cross-relation in the alto, so that *f♯* can then follow in ms. 3. Compare also 44*b* and *c*.

Modulation to the *mediant* region requires the neutralization of three tones: the 4th tone of the original region (*f* in C major) as well as the two natural tones of descending minor (*d* and *c*). In 45*b* this is accomplished by one descending scale line in mss. 3–4 of the tenor. In 45*c* observe the deceptive progression in ms. 7.

The neutralization before the appearance of the *subdominant* region is brought about simply by ascending with the leading tone of the tonic region (*b* in C major), as shown in mss. 2 and 3 of 46*a*. Notice that these examples are written in the meters of 3/2, 6/4 and 3/4, which should not be forgotten by the student.

The approach to the *dorian* region, like that to the mediant, requires the neutralization of three tones. In 47*b*, ms. 4, the tenor's *c♯* on the third beat makes the *d* of the alto a ninth. The tenor does not wait for the resolution but jumps to *a* making the *c♯* a tenth. In ms. 6 the tenor enters on the third beat as a fourth to the *f♯* of the alto, which is not incorrect as all these notes can be considered as passing notes. But the eighth note *d* which follows definitely improves the situation.

Exs. 48–51 illustrate modulations starting from a minor tonality. Notice that in moving to the *v–minor* region in 48*a* both the natural 6th (*f♮*) and substitute 6th (*f♯*) tones are neutralized, the former descending to the 5th tone, *e*, the latter ascending to the substitute 7th tone, *g♯*. The alternatives in ms. 4 provide greater rhythmic variety than the original. Observe also the unusual rhythm of the cambiata in ms. 3 which prevents the appearance of the seventh in parallel motion on the third beat (*f♯* to *e* above) that would have resulted if the usual rhythm in even quarter notes had been employed.

In 49*a*, which leads to the *subtonic*, there is a return in ms. 2 to the 7th tone of the descending scale which necessitates repetition of the substitute 7th tone. In 49*b*, *g♯*, the leading tone of *A* major, proceeds to *a* in ms. 5, but the tenor produces a deceptive progression with its *f♯*. In ms. 6, the tenor uses a characteristic eighth note figure which is very effective in keeping up the metrical movement. In 49*c*, ms. 2, the *f* of the tenor makes the *c* a suspension whose resolution would be a dim. 5. The interrupted resolution postpones the *b*, however, until the tenor has *g*, a sixth. The leading tone *a♮*, which is introduced in ms. 3, should really have appeared again in this example.

Ex. 50 leads to the *subdominant*. In 50*b*, ms. 8, the *c* of the alto is a dissonance on the first eighth note; the second eighth note makes it a consonance, but then the half note *g* on the second beat makes it a dissonance again. This *g* followed by an *f♯* offers in itself the aspect of a dissonance. In 50*c*, the modulation is brought about by the passing *f♭* in the bass (ms. 2).

In the examples leading to the *submediant* (Ex. 51) the modulations occur rather rapidly, but the lengthy cadences that follow definitely do establish the new regions.

A. from Major
Ex. 44 to Dominant region

a) C–G

b) Bb–F

c) A–E

Ex. 45 to mediant region

a) C–e

b) F–a

c) G–b

B. from Minor
Ex. 48 to v minor
a) a-e

b) f-c

c) c#-g#

Ex. 49 to Subtonic region
a) a-G

b) b-A

c) c-Bb

PART II

SIMPLE COUNTERPOINT IN THREE VOICES

I

FIRST SPECIES

Cantus firmus *and two added voices in whole notes*

GENERAL CONSIDERATIONS: CONSONANCES AND DISSONANCES
IN THREE VOICES

§ **102.** Counterpoint in three voices offers the possibility of producing full triads.

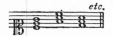

§ **103.** Triads may appear in first inversion—as 6-chords—but they may *not* appear in second inversion—as 6/4-chords—until further advice has been given.

§ **104.** It is always advantageous, though not necessary, to use full triads. A fluent and correct voice leading and treatment of dissonances, however, is more important. It may thus happen occasionally that all three voices meet in primes or octaves. Although this is not entirely wrong, it had better be reserved for beginnings and endings. As a general rule, however, either at least one consonant interval or a dissonance in the form of a *conventionalized formula* should be added to a prime or an octave.

§ **105.** If only one consonant interval is added, there are various possibilities for doubling the third voice, as can be seen from the following examples:

A. If the fifth is added to the lowest tone, either the lowest tone is doubled as in (1) or the fifth is doubled as in (2):

B. If the third is added to the lowest tone, either the lowest tone is doubled as in (1) or the third is doubled as in (2):

C. If the sixth is added to the lowest tone, either the lowest tone is doubled as in (1) or the sixth is doubled as in (2):

§ **106.** Consonant triads can be constructed on the various degrees of the major and minor scales in the aforementioned ways. The diminished triads on VII of major, and II, VI and VII of minor cannot be considered consonant, however, as the dissonant interval of diminished fifth (−5) appears above the lowest voice.

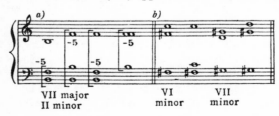

VII major
II minor

VI
minor

VII
minor

§ **107.** The diminished triad is *only* permitted as a consonance in the first inversion, where the consonant intervals of 6 and 3 appear above the lowest voice.

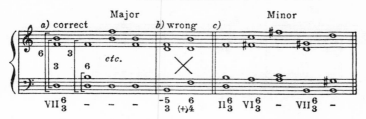

§ **108.** The augmented triad on III of minor is also considered dissonant because of the presence of a dissonant interval, the augmented fifth ($+5$), above the lowest voice.

§ **109.** The second inversion of triads, the 6/4-chord, is of course dissonant because of the presence of the interval of the 4 above the lowest voice.

§ **110.** However, these dissonant diminished and augmented triads, and 6/4-chords too, are often produced by passing notes or suspensions, as the following examples show:

HIDDEN PARALLELS IN THREE VOICES

§ **111.** The danger of open and hidden parallel 8s and 5s becomes greater, of course, the more voices there are involved. However, there may at the same time be greater tolerance for these hidden parallels, especially if only one of the voices is an outer one. As a matter of fact there are numerous cases where the greatest composers have not been afraid to use them. Such hidden 8s and 5s as those in the following example can hardly be excluded:

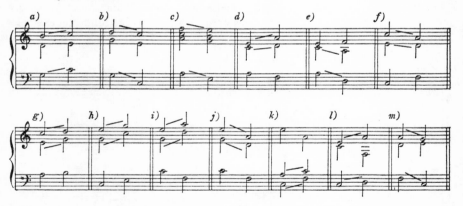

The worst cases of hidden parallel 8s are of the type shown in the following examples. These must be avoided absolutely because the note into which a passing or suspended dissonance has to move should never be taken in parallel movement by any other voice. The dissonance *must* land on that particular note, the other voice does not have to. Movement of the second voice on to it is unnecessary; and the ear would not acknowledge such movement.[1]

ADVICE AND DIRECTIONS FOR THE FIRST SPECIES

§ 112. Select three neighbouring voices such as soprano, alto and tenor, or alto, tenor and bass. Do not use such combinations as soprano, tenor and bass, or soprano, alto and bass.

The CF can be in the upper, middle or lower voice. If it is in the soprano, the alto and tenor will be added; if it is in the alto as highest voice, the tenor and bass will be added; if it is in the alto as middle voice, the soprano and tenor will be added, i.e. one above and one below the CF; if the CF is in the tenor as middle voice, the alto and bass will be added; if the CF is in the tenor as lowest voice, the soprano and alto will be added; and finally, if the CF is in the bass, the alto and tenor will be added.

[1] The student often arrives at emergencies in part leading where he does not know how to obey one rule without violating another or is forced to renounce a laudable achievement. As a teacher I have asked my students to mark such violations thus (+), indicating that they were aware of them. These I would then consider lesser evils.

COMMENT ON EXAMPLES IN FIRST SPECIES, EXS. 52 AND 53

It should be repeated that an incomplete harmony like that in ms. 3 of 52*a* need not be avoided (see § 104 and § 105). The same type of harmony occurs in 52*b*, ms. 3, and in many other examples. A succession of 6-chords, as in 52*b* and *c*, is also admissible. The 6-chords in 52*i*, however, progress for too long a time in consecutive parallel motion, and this is not to be recommended.

In the cadence the final tonic may be preceded by (1) V, as in 52*a*, *g*, *h* and *k*, (2) V6, as in 52*b*, *f* and *j*, or (3) VII6, as in 52*c*, *d*, *e* and *i*.

Other points to observe: as in first species in two voices, the repetition of tones is not wrong, least of all in middle voices (see 52*b* alto, 52*c* tenor, and other examples where the notes are tied). In 52*d*, however, the bass does perhaps stop for too long a time on one tone.

Hidden 5s occur in 52*g*, ms. 9, and 52*j*, ms. 7; they are almost unavoidable here. Compare § 111.

Melodic repetitions occur in 52*a* where the tenor voice produces monotony by bringing in *c* three times and *g* twice, and in 52*h* where the interval of a third appears three times in succession in the midst of an otherwise good example.

Examples in minor

The examples in minor (Ex. 53) suffer because of the severe demands of neutralization (see 'neutr.- - -' in examples). There is little variety in the harmony, and the voice leading is mostly monotonous. In 53*f* it is difficult to continue at all without violating one of the rules, if the *g* in the bass at ms. 4 is used. Perhaps one could use two half notes, as in the next series of examples, to improve the situation.

Ex. 52

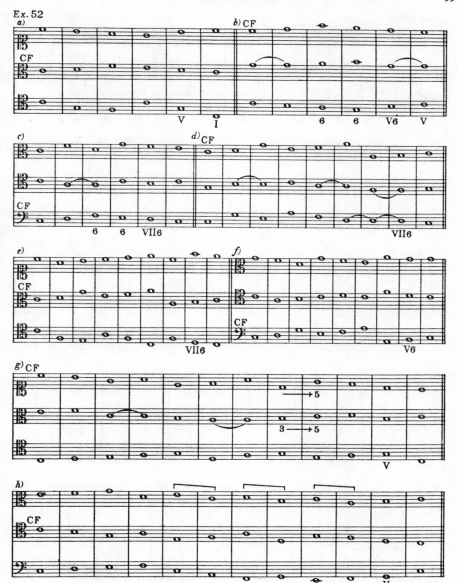

Ex. 52 (cont.)

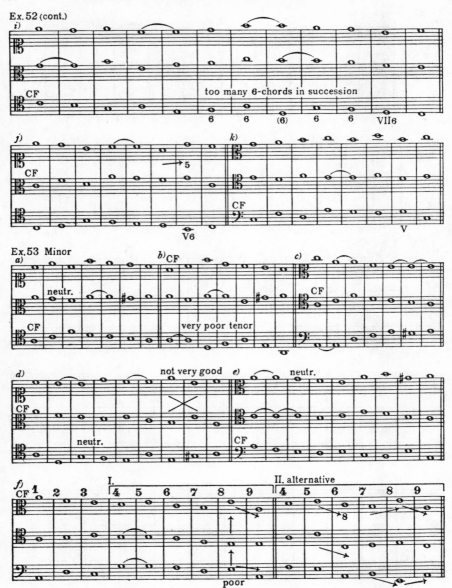

II

SECOND SPECIES

Two voices added to cantus firmus: *one in whole notes and one in half notes,*
or both in half notes

ADVICE AND DIRECTIONS

§ 113. In the first exercises in second species it is recommended that half notes be written in only one of the voices. There are thus the following possibilities in three voices:

Voices:	(1)	(2)	(3)	(4)	(5)	(6)
Upper:	CF	CF	○	♩	○	♩
Middle:	○	♩	CF	CF	♩	○
Lower:	♩	○	♩	○	CF	CF

§ 114. In the writing of half notes the same principles as those described for two voices (see §§ 15 ff.) should be followed. These are that consonances may be used on both strong and weak beats, and that the only dissonance should be the passing note on the weak beat.

§ 115. Full triads in root position or first inversion should appear as often as possible, if the voice leading does not suffer thereby (see § 104). If a full triad is not possible on the strong beat it is a good idea to bring in either the missing interval (see 1–7 below), or a tone which belongs to a different harmony (8–11 below), on the weak beat:

COMMENT ON EXAMPLES IN SECOND SPECIES, EXS. 54 AND 55

In some of the examples in second species (Exs. 54 and 55) it is necessary to use half notes in both voices in the penultimate measure (at ⊗) for there to be consonances on both beats. A perfect cadence—II–V–I—is produced in most cases as a consequence (54b, c, g and j). In 54d, on the other hand, the V is preceded by VII6 on the first half note, while in 54i the second half note is a passing dissonance leading to an ending on the third. Suspensions are used in the endings of 54k and l in anticipation of fourth species in order to avoid less satisfactory solutions, such as:

In 54c, the intermittent 5s in mss. 2–3 are tolerable—but these 5s are only tolerable in three voices, and not in two—because of the interval of the fourth in between.

In 54d the contour of the tenor is not very good. What is objectionable here is that first the tenor continues in the same direction after a leap (at □) and then a broken chord follows.

In 54e, ms. 2, the diminished triad in its first inversion (VII6) is introduced. Notice also its appearance in 54j, ms. 6, and in the penultimate measures of 54k and l.

In 54f two interesting passing notes occur. The first, in ms. 3, may not sound well on the piano as it is a second to the bass, but it is good in vocal writing. The second, in ms. 5, makes an augmented fourth.

Notice that some of the examples begin after a half note rest; this also happened in two-voice writing.

In minor (Ex. 55) the ending with two half notes presents difficulties whenever the leading tone (g♯ in A minor) appears on the first half note. This makes necessary the insertion between the 7th and 8th tones of another tone (e, the 5th tone or b, the 2nd), as in 55a, b and e (at ▱). In 55d, however, the only way out of this difficulty is to use a whole note (at ▭). In a few instances half notes are used in the second added voice (see 55a, d and e); this is primarily to facilitate voice leading.

Ex. 54

Ex.54 (cont.)

Ex.55 Minor

TWO VOICES IN HALF NOTES

§ 116. If two added voices move in half notes there is the danger that too many dissonances will meet simultaneously as for example at ×*a*, ×*b* and ×*c* of Ex. 56. Such dissonances need not be entirely excluded, although it is doubtful whether a beginner can take responsibility for them. The problem is best avoided by either not using two passing notes simultaneously or having one of the voices consonant with the CF. In the following example consonances occur in both voices in (*a*) and (*h*) (VII6); in (*b*) (6/4-chord), (*c*), (*f*) and (*g*), a passing note appears in only one of the voices; while simultaneous passing notes in both voices are found in (*d*), (*e*) and (*i*). The latter occur either in parallel motion (only thirds and sixths are permitted for this) or, and this is commoner, in contrary motion as in (*e*) and (*i*).

COMMENT ON EXAMPLES WITH TWO VOICES IN HALF NOTES, EXS. 56 AND 57

Passing notes are used in the various ways mentioned above; in some cases they will produce diminished triads in root position (56*a* at □) and in others 6/4-chords (56*a*, *b*, *c* and *d*). In 56*b*, ms. 5, the passing note *d* in the alto is dissonant to both other voices, and there is the unusual phenomenon of a tenor jumping in parallel motion to the tone *a*, which is a fourth with the alto. This tone, however, is consonant with the soprano, and so is correct. A similar case may be found in 56*c*, ms. 3, where the passing note *a* in the upper voice is also dissonant to both other voices. In 56*e*, ms. 9, the passing seventh produced by a tenor leap in parallel motion can be explained similarly.

Endings with both voices in half notes can usually have satisfactory changes of harmony on both beats. In both 56*d* and *e* there is a perfect cadence—II6–V–I. An ending in 56*c*, however, is difficult, if not impossible, because of the leading tone in the bass, the CF. Only one harmony, V6, can be expressed in this case. As the following shows, none of the solutions are very satisfactory:

Though contrary motion is in general of a higher order, parallel motion need not be excluded entirely if it does not last for too long a time. Thus the parallel 3s of 56e, mss. 7–8 for example, are quite good, but perhaps there is too much parallel motion of both 3s and 6s in 56b and f.

In 56a, ms. 4, the outer voices leap simultaneously: this is distinctly bad, particularly as hidden 5s are produced, though it would be difficult to find another solution.

In minor (Ex. 57) the usual problems of neutralization arise, especially at the ending. In 57a, for example, the following use of the substitute 6th tone, f♯, would have been possible in the penultimate measure, if the f♮ (X) had been neutralized:

But the suspended a resolving into the leading tone g♯ has had to be used instead. A similar case occurs in 57b where the unneutralized 6th tone in the soprano, ms. 3 (X), makes it necessary to use the suspended 6/5-chord instead of the substitute 6th tone as shown in the alternative. In 57c the leading tone is avoided entirely, though the V–I of the cadence is still expressed. In 57d the final V is even introduced as a passing 6/4-chord. Finally, in 57e the substitute 6th tone could be introduced in the penultimate measure in place of the suspension shown here, although the alto voice leaves much to be desired in either case.

Ex.56

III

THIRD SPECIES

Addition of four quarter notes to a cantus firmus *and whole notes or half notes in the third voice*

ADVICE AND DIRECTIONS

§ **117.** The advice given in third species for two voices regarding quarter notes is also applicable here (see §§ 24 ff.). Dissonances must be treated according to the first and second conventionalized formulas, i.e. passing notes and cambiatas. But it is self-evident that consonances must conform to the considerations to be observed in three-voice writing.

§ **118.** There are two variants of this species: in the first, which is a little easier, the third voice proceeds in whole notes; in the second, the third voice moves in half notes. It is little use trying quarter notes in both voices for the moment. The first variant is illustrated in Exs. 58 and 59, the second in Exs. 60 and 61.

COMMENT ON EXAMPLES IN THIRD SPECIES, EXS. 58–61

In both 58*a* and 58*c* the third voice has two half notes in the penultimate measure. Other possible solutions for 58*a* are as follows:

In minor the use of half notes in the ending is necessary even more often because of the severe rules of neutralization. Half notes may even become necessary in the middle of an example, as in ms. 4 of 59*a*. In ms. 5 of the same example two successive dissonances appear. Because doubling the leading tone, *g♯*, is not possible, there remain only two tones which can be used—*e* and *b*. These, however, would produce a poor melody as the following shows:

Perhaps the only way out of this dilemma is to avoid the *g♯* altogether, and use *g♮* instead for two measures then neutralize it in the following measures, as shown here:

In mss. 7 and 8 of 59*c* the repetition of the three tones *e–f♯–g♯* in the tenor can be avoided in the following ways:

In the variant of this species where the third voice is written in half notes throughout (Exs. 60 and 61), the student must again be careful in the use of passing half notes. Notice them particularly in 60*b*, mss. 1, 5 and 7; 60*c*, ms. 3; and 61*b*, ms. 3.

The tenor's whole note in the penultimate measure of 60*a* can be avoided if the voices move as follows from ms. 6:

Suspensions have been used prematurely in 60c. The following example shows how they can be avoided:

The intermittent 5s in ms. 9 of 60c are not intolerable because the movement of the quarter notes constantly changes their harmonic meaning. But they can be avoided as the preceding example shows.

Several syncopations and suspensions appear in the minor examples; these will be explained more fully in fourth species. The dissonances in mss. 7 and 8 of 61a, in particular, require further explanation.

Ex.58

Ex. 60 (cont.)

Ex. 61 Minor

IV

FOURTH SPECIES

Addition of syncopated half notes to a cantus firmus and whole notes, half notes or quarter notes in the third voice

ADVICE AND DIRECTIONS

§ **119.** There are several variants possible in this species in that the third added voice can be written in whole notes, half notes or quarter notes, or even in syncopations and mixed notes. It is recommended that the student tries exercises in whole notes and quarter notes first before attempting anything further.

§ **120.** As in two-voice writing (see §§ 36 ff.) the syncopation must begin as a consonance on the weak beat, the second half note being either a consonance, or a suspension whose resolution follows immediately.

§ **121.** If the second half note is a consonance, cases like the following will result:

§ **122.** Intermittent 8s or 5s like those in the following example should be avoided:

The movement of the third voice in half notes or quarter notes, however, is usually capable of hiding these intermittent parallels (see 64*a*, mss. 6–7).

SUSPENSIONS IN THREE VOICES

§ **123.** A suspension requires:

(*a*) A preparation that is consonant with both the other voices, and

(*b*) A resolution that is consonant in the same manner, i.e. that produces a full triad or 6-chord, or is otherwise consonant with both the other voices.

A number of cases of suspensions are illustrated in the following examples:

§ **124.** As in two voices, one must avoid anticipating the tone onto which a seventh resolves. See (*j*) of the preceding example, which is incorrect. Strict counterpoint forbids even the use of the tone onto which a ninth resolves, in the middle and lower voices, as in (*n*). But if there is good voice leading this may be tolerated.

§ **125.** Intermittent parallel 8s and 5s following suspensions should in most cases be avoided. They often occur in the following ways:

These intermittent parallels may perhaps be tolerated, however, if one of the voices involved is a middle part, especially when more than three voices are employed and a rich change of harmony results.

But such complicated cases had better be avoided by the student to begin with.

COMMENT ON EXAMPLES IN FOURTH SPECIES, EXS. 62 AND 63

In 62a, ms. 3, the suspension b (at ⊗) is a second to the alto's a. This is quite correct for voices, even though it would not sound well on the piano.

In the ending of 62a the advantages of the suspension become evident. In 62b, however, although the syncopation has to be abandoned, a good ending is still possible. In 62c the ending requires the use of half notes in the upper voice (ms. 6).

In 63a, the first of the minor examples, use of VII of A-minor as a 6-chord in ms. 7 gives a fair ending. The alternative here, however, is even more interesting because in the penultimate measure (at ⊗) there appears an augmented triad which no theorist would forbid. Interesting also from the standpoint of rich harmony is the ending of 63c where both the c♯ and d♯ change their harmonic meaning within the measure. An attempt in 63d to make the alto more interesting ends catastrophically in ms. 4 because the d cannot be neutralized.

Ex. 62

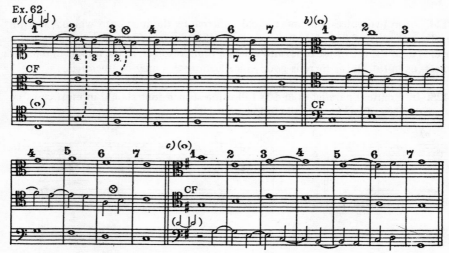

SYNCOPATIONS WITH ADDED VOICE IN HALF NOTES OR QUARTER NOTES

§ **126.** A variant of fourth species is to write the added voice in half notes or quarter notes. Movement of this voice during a suspension onto a tone consonant with the resolution (cf. § 89) will then occur, as in Ex. 64 where only quarter notes are used.

SUSPENSIONS AS SEVENTH CHORDS AND THEIR INVERSIONS

§ **127.** Seventh chords and their inversions are often brought about by such suspensions in three-part writing. They are usually resolved in conjunction with movement in the third voice. Harmonically these chords can be explained as follows—they are shown here (with their resolutions) as V7–I:

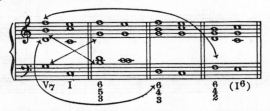

The same treatment can be applied to the II degree:

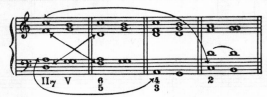

One can thus regard the appearance of the inversions 6/5, 4/3 and 2 as being due to the mere interchanging of upper voices and bass.

§ **128.** In the following examples in three voices suspensions occur as seventh chords and their inversions, the added voice being in half notes. Notice that the added voice must move into the resolution in order for it to be consonant. In the 4/3 suspension both voices have to be suspended as they are both dissonant to the CF.

§ 129. Quarter notes are used in the following example rather as half notes are in the preceding one. The resolution of the suspension always occurs on the third beat, but the second quarter note is either a passing note ((*a*) and (*b*)) or a tone consonant with the CF, as in (*c*), (*e*) and (*f*). An interrupted resolution appears in (*d*) where both voices are written in mixed notes.

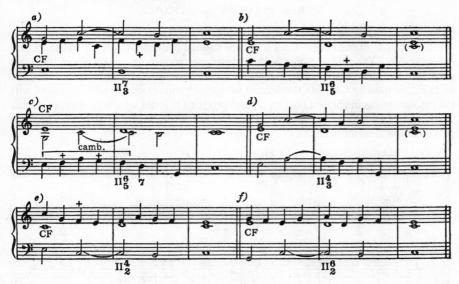

§ 130. Suspensions of the same kind are illustrated in minor in the following examples:

As in some of the preceding examples, suspensions sometimes appear in both voices, particularly with the 4/3-chord. In (*f*) all three voices move together in the first measure; this procedure is actually more characteristic of cadences without CF (see Chapter VI).

OTHER TYPES OF SUSPENSION

§ **131.** Other types of suspension, including 5/4, 5/2, 6/2 and 3/2 ones, and also resolutions into chords other than those mentioned previously, appear in the following examples. The added voice, which sometimes moves in mixed notes too, may contain during the suspension: (1) only tones consonant with the CF, as in (*a*), (*e*) and (*f*); (2) passing notes on the second beat which move onto tones consonant with the resolution, as in (*b*), (*c*), (*i*), (*k*), (*l*) and (*m*); or (3) tones which are part of a cambiata, as in (*g*), (*h*) and (*j*). In (*d*) an interrupted resolution is used to continue the movement in quarter notes.

§ **132.** Similar suspensions in minor are illustrated in the examples that follow. In (*e*) and (*f*) (at ⊗) all three voices move into the resolution. Although this cannot be done with a CF, suspensions are in fact often treated this way (see Cadences Without Cantus Firmus (Chapter VI)).

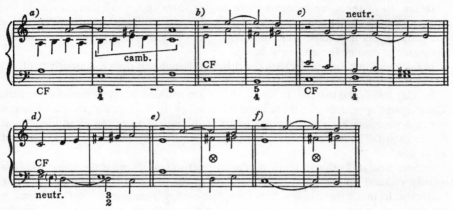

COMMENT ON SUSPENSIONS WITH ADDED VOICE IN QUARTER NOTES, EXS. 64 AND 65

Fluent movement in the added voices should always be the main concern. Whether or not they produce a full triad, and whether or not they change the harmonic meaning within the measure, is of lesser importance, though full triads and changes of harmonic meaning do contribute greatly to the quality of the examples. In ms. 1 of 64*a* the tone *c* of the CF changes its harmonic meaning twice through the *a* of the tenor and the *e–f* of the alto. And in the first half of ms. 2 the alto similarly gives the *b* of the CF a double meaning. On the third beat there is no complete triad; the passing note *f* in the alto, however, compensates satisfactorily for this slight shortcoming. In ms. 4 the harmony remains colourless in the second half, though it was very impressive in the first half. The absence of a suspension in ms. 9 is compensated for by the interesting movement in the alto; if there is a weakness here one could consider it to be in the tenor's anticipation of the *g* in the CF. This measure is also not very good because all three voices descend, and do not entirely avoid intermittent 5s in the process. The alternative for the penultimate measure shows a good way of avoiding the consecutive dissonances in the alto.

In 64*b*, ms. 3, all three voices have *b♭* on the third beat. This had better be avoided, and the alternative used instead. Ms. 8 illustrates the solution to an interesting problem. While the alto is preparing the *e♭* in ms. 7 to become a suspension resolving onto *d* in ms. 8, the bass also has an *e♭* (on the fourth beat of ms. 7); and it moves from this down to *d* on the first beat of ms. 8. Were the bass to remain on this *d* it would produce parallel 8s. But in fact when the *d* appears in the alto, the bass has already moved down to *b♭*.

In ms. 10 of the same example there appear three successive dissonances in the bass: a seventh to the tenor, a fourth to the alto and a diminished fifth to the tenor respectively. As it is impossible to consider all three as passing notes it would be necessary to change the alto as indicated.

In 64*c* the upper voice ends with the third. Although this does not strictly conform to the rules it need not be avoided.

In 65*a*, ms. 3, the manner in which the 5s are avoided in the soprano is correct. The frequent appearance of the natural 7th tone, *g♮*, in the soprano makes its return in ms. 6 necessary for the neutralization. But the repetition of the *g♯* in mss. 7 and 8 is awkward. The first alternative is a poor solution to this problem, and the second a fair one.

In 65*c*, mss. 1–2, the soprano moves in intermittent 5s with the tenor. This is usually excused on the grounds that the *a♭* in the soprano is a tone of the same harmony. In ms. 5 there is illustrated another escape from intermittent 5s. In ms. 6 the cambiata moves in an interesting way from a ninth into a consonance with the resolution of the soprano.

Ex. 64

V

FIFTH SPECIES

Addition of mixed notes in one or two voices to the cantus firmus

ADVICE AND DIRECTIONS

§ 133. Three variants of fifth species are illustrated in the following examples. In Ex. 66 only one of the added voices carries mixed notes; the other has whole notes. In Ex. 67 mixed notes are combined with syncopations. In Ex. 68 both added voices move in mixed notes.

§ 134. There are no new rules for this species. The inclusion of conventionalized formulas should not be overlooked, and their treatment should be reviewed in two and three voices. And the rules of rhythmic restriction should be preserved (see §§ 48 ff.), as well as those concerning the neutralization of turning-points in minor (§§ 64 ff.). Unneutralized tones are marked × in the examples, while their neutralization is marked *neutr*.

In the following examples the principal conventionalized formulas—passing notes (+), cambiatas (camb.), suspensions (susp.), and interrupted resolutions (⊗)—are shown, and also movement during suspensions (□).

COMMENT ON EXAMPLES IN FIFTH SPECIES, EXS. 66–68

In 66*a*, ms. 5, the leap of the octave in the alto might be avoided in the way shown in the alternative; the alternative would avoid the leap to the tripled *g* in ms. 4, too.

In 67*a*, ms. 7, the resolution of the suspension in the soprano occurs on the second beat while the alto is still suspended, the latter not resolving until the fourth beat.

In 67*b*, ms. 2, there is an example of the suspended 6/5-chord discussed in the preceding chapter (§§ 127 ff.).

In 68*a*, ms. 1, the entrance of the soprano doubling the note *a* to which the tenor has moved is not very good, although it provides a good melodic line.

In 68*b*, ms. 2, the descending 7th tone of minor, *d*♮, is doubled in the alto—where the 6th tone then follows as a passing note. In the same measure the alto also passes through two dissonances with its two eighth notes—the fourth *b* and the dim.5 *c*. This is not entirely wrong, but there are probably too many questionable events in one measure. In ms. 7 the tenor moves first into a passing dissonance against the bass, and then into one against the alto from which it leaps. This also is a little too free.

Ex. 66 Mixed Notes and Whole Notes

F

Ex. 68 (cont.)

VI

THIRD COMPOSITIONAL APPLICATION: CADENCES WITHOUT *CANTUS FIRMUS*

GENERAL CONSIDERATIONS

§ 135. The advice for producing cadences without CF in two voices given in §§ 72 ff., is also valid for cadences in three voices. The procedure can be the same: always make one of the voices overlap the others for a measure or more; consider the contour of the voice carefully; use long notes frequently, especially when they prepare syncopations; and finally, add two good counter-melodies. Let one of the voices then overlap the others again, and proceed as before until an opportunity for an ending is in view.

§ 136. Such segments are somewhat longer than ordinary cadential segments. But as long as they fulfil the most important task of a cadence, i.e. the expression and establishment of a tonality, they deserve the name of cadence.

§ 137. As a preliminary exercise the student is recommended to add third voices (upper, middle or lower) to good examples in two voices, using either examples which have been given in this treatise or some he has made up himself. In using examples in two voices it will often be necessary to change one of the clefs or both, and sometimes even to transpose the voices to another tonality, to find space for an added voice.

ADVICE FOR THE TREATMENT OF ADDED VOICES

§ 138. Independence of voices is an aesthetically founded obligation in contrapuntal writing. Having selected a certain number of voices, a composer should prove as often as possible that his choice was correct. In every composition there will be places where not all the voices are necessary. When this happens one or more of them will rest. But if a voice is singing or playing it must be adding something necessary, and this it has to do on its own.

§ 139. The fact that a voice is participating has to be noticeable. One of the best means to this end is rhythmic differentiation. Exaggerating this advice a little, one could say that when one voice moves the other should not: when one voice moves in small notes the other should not do the same—it should use longer notes instead. Simultaneous movement should be avoided.

These rules are of course too strict, and contradictions to them can be found very often. Although at times it obscures the contours of the voices, simultaneous movement does not destroy independence entirely. On the other hand, rhythmic independence will always be effective.

§ 140. One of the requirements which an added voice must fulfil is that of making the harmony richer and fuller. Of first importance is the fact that empty colourless harmonies will become more definite with certain additions, as for instance when a third, fifth or sixth is added to an empty octave, or a third to an empty fifth, or a fifth or sixth to a third, etc. We must not forget about passing notes and other dissonances, either.

§ 141. This exercise in adding voices has been introduced here as preparation for a task which will occur more frequently the closer this course approaches compositional problems. The writing of chorale preludes and the addition of voices to fugue themes, for instance, require the ability to do this.

§ 142. In the following examples, first various given intervals are shown with added consonances (a–e); and then prepared suspensions (f–m) and passing notes (n–t) are illustrated:

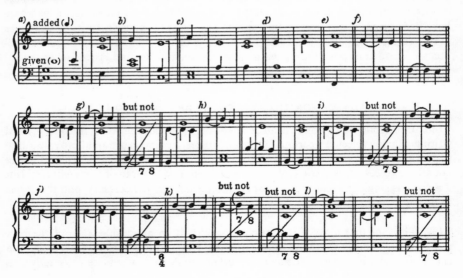

COMMENT ON EXAMPLES WITH ADDED VOICES, EXS. 69-71

In Ex. 69 third voices are added in three different positions to the two-voiced examples of 40*a* (see p. 79)—in the middle (69*a*), at the bottom (69*b*) and on top (69*c*). Similar treatment is accorded to 40*b* in the examples of Ex. 70, and to 40*g–l* in the examples in minor of Ex. 71.

The addition of third voices makes possible frequent harmonic changes, as for instance in ms. 2 of 69*a*. In ms. 5 the interrupted resolution is treated as a change of harmony—a change of harmony in that the interrupting tone *a* (at ⊗) is consonant with both voices. The real resolution *d* makes the *c* of the alto a prepared dissonance.

In 69*b*, ms. 2, there occurs a treatment of the dissonance which has not been used with smaller notes before. The *b* of the soprano is made a seventh on the last beat by the tenor's *c*.

One can see how different the harmony can become when the position of the added voice is changed, by comparing the three versions of ms. 2 in Ex. 69.

In 70*a* the added voice is monotonous because its compass is too narrow. In addition, the *f* in the alto in ms. 3 is hardly admissible as it is a dim. 5. A possible correction is shown in the alternative.

The added voice in 70*b* which is transposed to B♭, is much less monotonous, though monotony would not be as bad in the middle voice as it would in the upper. And in 70*c* where it is the lowest voice, it contains enough variety to function as a good bass, which is always a merit.

All the examples in minor (Ex. 71) are a little longer because of the need for neutralization of every 7th or 6th tone in every voice before substitutes can appear.

Thus in 71a the tenor's c in ms. 5, and its d in ms. 6 (⊗) require a return to the same tones in ms. 8 for neutralization to take place. The tenor here is a little too low.

In 71b, ms. 1, the d♯ in the alto is questionable. The passing note g♯ in the bass, which is a fourth to the tenor, is the cause of the problem.

There is no reason why the added voice should not move in added 3s or 6s with one of the other voices occasionally, as in ms. 5 of 71b. This, however, should not be taken too far. In general the addition of 3s or 6s is reserved for some form of double counterpoint where voices are constructed to admit them.

After ms. 1, the added voice in 71c only uses tones of the descending minor scale, and thus sounds as if it were in E♭ major. In some cases this might be an advantage, but as a general rule it is better for every voice to have the characteristics of minor. The f in the alto, ms. 8, is best excused as a passing note on the strong beat.

In 71d, ms. 2, one meets again the rapid change from ascending substitutes to tones of the descending scale encountered in 71a, mss. 4–5. The added voice of 71d has an ugly repetition in mss. 4 and 5 and does not even get rid of the repeated g in ms. 6.

In 71e the soprano is so low in mss. 5 and 6 that the f of the alto in ms. 4 cannot be neutralized. This may be excused where another voice, here the soprano in ms. 5, performs a neutralization in the same register.

The syncopation of the first measure of 71f is questionable because a syncopation should begin on a strong beat. However, this rule is too strict for it to be possible to overcome the difficulties of neutralization. The alternative, 71g, is given because the position of the tenor limits free movement in the other voices.

Ex.69 Addition of a Third Voice to Cadences of Ex.40

(original changed)

CADENCES WITHOUT GIVEN VOICES

§ **143.** As it is always the best procedure in dealing with cadences without given voices to use syncopations—preferably suspensions—as often as possible in one of the voices, it might be of some help to consider a number of ways in which suspensions can be treated first of all. Notice particularly in the following examples the interrupted resolutions (marked ⊗) and the movement in one or both of the voices during the suspensions (marked ☐). Parallel 3s and 6s occur in some of the examples (*g, h, i, t* and *v*), sometimes during the suspensions.

COMMENT ON CADENCES WITHOUT GIVEN VOICES, EXS. 72 AND 73

Following recommended procedure, one should begin with a long note and tie it over as a preparation for a suspension—as in the soprano of 72a. The contents of the first three measures are provided in this way. In mss. 4 and 5 the tenor acts similarly— like a CF. In 72b it is the bass which assumes this role during the first two measures; the alto and tenor then have syncopations. The movement of the other two voices is regulated according to the advice given for all the species in which smaller notes have to be added to longer ones.

Rhythmic variation should, if possible, be brought into all three voices; it is definitely a merit. It is good, then, that all of the examples at least begin with different rhythms. In the course of examples, however, the 'tendency of the smallest notes' may become predominant in all voices. Still at least one of the voices, such as the tenor in 72a, ms 4, or 72b, ms. 6, for instance, ought to have more outspoken independence. It can also be recommended that at least one of the voices should enter after a rest, as in 73b and 73c.

Ex.73 Minor

× = not neutralized

VII

FOURTH COMPOSITIONAL APPLICATION: CADENCES TO VARIOUS REGIONS; MODULATION

ADVICE AND DIRECTIONS

§ **144.** The advice previously given for modulation in two voices (§§ 90 ff.) is also applicable for that in three voices. The only new difficulty derives from the need to neutralize the three voices. An escape from this obligation can be obtained if one of the voices is made to avoid cross-related tones as much as possible. This is occasionally difficult when the goal is a minor tonality. In modulating from C major to its mediant, e minor, for instance, there are three potential cross-related tones: f, d and c. As all of them can be neutralized by descending, there is the danger that voices will reach too low a register and also use descending scales too often.

The rules for neutralization of cross-related tones have been given in a manner that is far too strict to allow freedom of voice leading. In textbooks based on the style of Palestrina these restrictions are less sharp, but they do not lead, however, to the development of a harmony which employs a greater number of substitute tones. Many of the examples given at this stage are stiff, unnatural, overdone, monotonous and too long as a consequence of the requirements of neutralization. Often a correct solution is almost impossible. However, facing a problem and recognizing its difficulty is often of greater value than finding an easy solution. And so this treatise will continue with this strict treatment. Advice for freer treatment will be given later, but it is only for students who have developed a sense of balance as a result of these exercises—which aim for a thorough ear training.

§ **145.** Once again a preliminary exercise similar to that in two voices, based upon a CF which modulates (see § 100, Ex. 43), might prove useful. In Ex. 74 an upper and lower voice are added to two CFs in mixed notes previously given in § 100.

§ **146.** In Ex. 75 third voices are added to two voice examples chosen from Exs. 44–51. Modulations to the following regions take place: to the dominant, mediant, subdominant, and dorian, from major tonalities; and to the five-minor, subtonic, subdominant, and submediant, from minor tonalities.

COMMENT ON MODULATIONS TO RELATED REGIONS, EXS. 74 AND 75

In 74*b* the stopping of the quarter note movement in ms. 6 is unsatisfactory.

In ms. 4 of 75*a* the passing note *f♯* in the tenor and the interrupting tone in the soprano (⊗) meet with the *g* of the alto on the second beat. This might sound harsh but it is not incorrect.

In 75*b*, ms. 6, a situation appears for which it is difficult to find a solution. Tenor and alto leap an octave in parallel 5s. But as it is the same 5 one need not regard this as a case of parallel motion. So the leap by the two voices might be tolerated, especially as it is difficult to find a more satisfactory solution.

In ms. 2 of 75*c* the *c♯* of the soprano is not neutralized (at X). Accordingly the *c♮* on the last beat of the tenor gives a strong impression of cross-relation.

75*d* contains a number of cambiatas which, entering at different points with one another, produce the impression of imitation (to be discussed more fully in Chapter X). The soprano and tenor in ms. 6 of this example move by parallel motion into a fifth on the third beat. This parallel motion in the two outer voices is questionable, especially as the *b♭* appears too soon after the *b♮*. The *c* of the alto in ms. 2 (X) is left unneutralized, but it reappears in the same register in the soprano in ms. 5, and is neutralized there (*neutr.*).

In 75*e* the original tonality, *a* minor, lasts three full measures, and then, in ms. 4, the modulation occurs too suddenly. Although the *c* of the alto is correctly neutralized, the *c♯* of the bass on the third beat is a little surprising.

The alto in the first three measures of 75*f* uses the same rhythmical pattern three times. It also contains too many leaps.

In 75*g* the alto begins below the tenor, a consequence of its imitation of the bass. It was mentioned earlier that a modulation from *C* major to *d* minor (its dorian region) necessitated the neutralization of three tones. Here, the application of substitute 6th and 7th tones has had to be postponed because the *b♭* has been introduced first. Nevertheless it would be quite possible to neutralize the *b♭* itself sooner and then bring in the *b♮* and *c♯*.

In 75*h* the *e* of the alto in ms. 2 becomes a prepared suspension on the second quarter note, but is resolved correctly. The modulation sounds premature here because the *b♮* in the alto in ms. 1 is not neutralized.

Ex.74 from Major to Minor *(sm)* (F-d)

from Minor to Major *(M)* (e-G)

Ex.75 from Major: to Dominant region (C-G) (from Ex. 44*a*)

to mediant region (C-e) (from Ex. 45*a*)

to Subdominant region (D-G) (from Ex. 46*b*)

Ex. 75 (cont.) to dorian region (C–d) (from Ex. 47a)

from Minor: to v-minor region (a–e) (from Ex. 48a)

to Subtonic region (a–G) (from Ex. 49a)

to subdominant region (a–d) (from Ex. 50a)

to Submediant region (a–F) (from Ex. 51a)

MODULATIONS WITHOUT GIVEN VOICES

§ **147.** Modulations without given voices to various regions in both major and minor are presented in Ex. 76. All of the previous considerations regarding modulation in three voices are observed.

COMMENT ON MODULATIONS WITHOUT GIVEN VOICES, EX. 76

The leap of a minor sixth in ms. 2 of the alto in 76a is allowed by some theorists. It is evident however, why it had better be avoided here. The soprano has to resolve its *b* onto *a*; the movement of the alto is then quite ineffectual because its *a* disappears behind the necessary *a* of the soprano. It is thus difficult to find a satisfactory solution at this point.

In 76d, ms. 4, the movement of the alto can only be explained in terms of its similarity to that found in some of the conventionalized formulas (the cambiata, for example). The cause of this movement is the rule that the 7th tone, *b♮*, must be followed by the 8th tone, *c*. To try a solution like that of alternative 1 would not help because of the very bad afterbeating primes with the soprano it would entail. The other solution (alternative 2) would produce parallel 5s with the tenor. The original form at least avoids wrong parallels.

In ms. 5 of the same example a progression (V–VI) is used which is usually known as the 'deceptive cadence'. In this treatise the phrase 'deceptive *progression*' will be used instead, because the term *cadence* should be preserved for its real function.

In 76e, ms. 3, the passing note *b♮* in the tenor is a little harsh appearing, as it does, so soon after the characteristics of *d* minor, and also because it is a major ninth against the *c* of the alto.

Ex.76 to Dominant region (D-A)
a)

to mediant region (G-b)
b)

Ex. 76 (cont.)

VIII

FIFTH COMPOSITIONAL APPLICATION: INTERMEDIARY REGIONS

ADVICE AND DIRECTIONS

§ **148.** Modulations, even in smaller forms, often lead to one segment or section, or more, in which a *region* of the tonality is distinctly established. After a time these regions are usually abandoned and give way to other regions or to a return to the tonic region. This is the reason for calling them *intermediary regions*. Their purpose is usually that of emphasizing a contrast through their harmonic differences. This is achieved by using the characteristics of these regions more or less as if they themselves were basic tonalities.

§ **149.** The possibilities with regard to these intermediary regions are shown in this treatise in two ways: (1) by the actual insertion of one or more regions in an establishing manner in examples (see §§ 152 ff., Exs. 77–80); (2) by the use of the characteristics of a region in a more transitory way without its being established (see §§ 156, Ex. 81).

§ **150.** The examples in two and three voices containing cadences to various regions (Part I, Chapter VIII, and Part II, Chapter VII) need not have ended with modulations but could have been continued with a return to the tonic region, or even with movement to another region and then a return to the tonic. Of course, if these regions are only passing events they should not be dwelt on too long.

§ **151.** It is clear that only the most closely related regions should be included in these simple examples—that is, those indicated in the chart of the regions in Chapter VIII, Part I (§ 93). Deviation from the tonic region is the consequence of using tones other than those of the tonic. Even within the overtones of the tonic itself, however, there is a tendency towards the realization of this deviation. Every 5th (*G*) of a tone (*C*) aims for supremacy, i.e. it aims to become a tonic itself. The same is true of the other tones; when they finally succeed the result is usually a change of region. In other words, the harmonic density of a piece of music is determined by the tones of which it is composed.

Simple contrapuntal examples like the following ones, then, will not require remote deviations from the tonic. Such deviations are the result of the use of remotely related tones in the theme itself. It is further recommended that the intermediary regions in the examples be no more than two to four measures long.

§ **152.** If only one intermediary region appears in an example it will either be: (1) submediant (*sm*)—e.g. *a* minor from the tonic (*T*) *C* major; (2) dominant (*D*)—i.e. *G* major; (3) mediant (*m*)—i.e. *e* minor; (4) subdominant (*SD*)—i.e. *F* major; or (5) dorian (*dor*)—i.e. *d* minor. Examples of each of these regions followed by a return to the tonic region (*T*) are given in Ex. 77.

§ **153.** In a minor tonality, *a* minor for instance, the various closely related regions are: (1) mediant (*M*)—*C* major; (2) five-minor (*v*)—*e* minor; (3) subtonic (*subT*)— *G* major; (4) subdominant (*sd*)—*d* minor; (5) submediant (*SM*)—*F* major; and (6) dominant (*D*)—*E* major. Most of these regions are illustrated in Ex. 78.

COMMENT ON EXAMPLES WITH INTERMEDIARY REGIONS, EXS. 77 AND 78

The five examples of Ex. 77 begin with the same two measures. The continuation of each employs one of the regions listed in § 152. Symbols for the regions appear above the examples. Neutralization of cross-related tones between the regions is also shown (*neutr.* - - -).

It is remarkable that the single beginning admits of so many different continuations without imbalance. The final cadences (*cad.*) are short and must be strong accordingly, that is, they must produce many of the characteristics of scale lines and cadential harmonies. Thus in ms. 4 of 77*a* the alto moves scalewise thereby making full triads with the soprano and the tenor. On the third beat the *c* of the soprano is given a new meaning and this makes the leading tone *b* obligatory as the resolution of a suspension.

In 78a the appearance of the mediant region (*M*) is not very effective because every minor tonality has segments in its descending scale where no characteristics of minor appear.

Despite the fact that 78*b* uses many eighth notes, it remains rather stiff. In addition, the region of subtonic (*subT*) is only fleetingly presented.

The subdominant region (*sd*) in 78*c* is more impressive as a deviation from the tonic region. In mss. 5 and 6 both the tenor and the alto are rather high in register and a little unbalanced. The last eighth note in ms. 5 of the alto produces an augmented triad; although the voice leading is correct, this produces a strange effect in the context.

In 78*d*, ms. 5, the rules do not protect one entirely. The movement of the alto and tenor is not incorrect in practice; but this parallel movement from an aug. 4 into a perf. 4 is not recommended in strict counterpoint.

In 78*e* the presentation of the dominant region (*D*) should be more thorough. The dominant is, of course, closely related to the tonic, but a major region on the fifth degree in minor is more remote. Mss. 4 and 5 therefore sound a little unprepared. However, the return to the tonic region is convincing because the major chord on *E* functions here as a real dominant.

Ex. 77 Major

Ex. 78 Minor

TWO OR MORE INTERMEDIARY REGIONS IN AN EXAMPLE

§ **154.** In Exs. 79 and 80 two intermediary regions are brought in. This admits of much variety. After *sm*, for instance, there could follow *D* or *dor* or *SD*, etc., and after *dor* there could follow *SD*, etc. Thus many variations are possible; it is because after the first intermediary region there is always a choice of three or four other regions.

§ **155.** In selecting the second intermediary region it is recommended that such combinations as *m* and *SD*, regions which are only remotely related to each other, should be avoided. One can always determine how remote a region is by considering it as if it were a tonality. In this particular case one finds that the mediant—*e* minor in *C* major, which belongs as relative minor to the realm of the dominant, *G* major—is two fifths distant from the subdominant, *F* major. This is traditionally considered a rather remote relationship, and it would cause at least some difficulties.

COMMENT ON EXAMPLES WITH TWO OR MORE INTERMEDIARY
REGIONS, EXS. 79 AND 80

In 79*a*, ms. 4, it seems as though the resolution of a suspension is leading upwards in the tenor; the syncopated *f♯*, however, is not a dissonance. This is a very fluent example, though it is not the best procedure to begin with two voices after a quarter note rest.

79*e* passes through four regions and is very rich in harmonic content; all the transitions between regions are quite smooth, nevertheless. The *b♭* in the bass of ms. 8 is striking, but it is not too harsh.

In 80*a*, in minor, a move from *SM* to *D* is ventured. It is facilitated by the sustained *e* in ms. 5 of the tenor, which at once suggests the dominant. The subsequent scalewise procedure in all three voices strengthens this impression. Thus on the third beat the 6-chord on g♯ gives the effect of the tonic of a region. Two endings are provided: the first returns to the tonic region of *a* minor; the second modulates to the mediant region, *C* major.

80*b* and 80*c* likewise end in different regions from those with which they began.

SUBSTITUTE TONES AND ENRICHED CADENCES

§ 156. 81*a*, *b* and *c* use substitute tones pertaining to various regions after adequate neutralization—without ever establishing one of these regions. Instead, they only use the characteristics of these regions. 81*a* and *b* employ such means to produce modulations—that is, to bring about endings in regions other than those with which they began—while 81*c* is merely an enriched cadence.

Ex. 81 Using Substitute Tones

IX

SIXTH COMPOSITIONAL APPLICATION: IMITATION IN TWO AND THREE VOICES

GENERAL CONSIDERATIONS: TYPES OF IMITATION

§ **157.** One can consider imitation as a first attempt at connecting voices with each other by means other than those permitted by harmony. It is probably the first step towards working with motifs, too. However, whatever imitation may have meant to those composers who introduced this procedure in their music, it differs essentially from the employment of the motif in homophonic music. Repetition and motivic variation, leading to the creation of new motif forms which admit of connexion, produce the material of homophonic music. For this reason I call this style the style of *developing variation*.

§ **158.** In contrapuntal composition, on the other hand, motivic variation appears but rarely, and then its purpose is never that of producing new motivic forms. The types of motivic variation which are admissible here, such as the *comes* in fugue, and augmentation, diminution and inversion, do not aim at development but only at producing variety of sound by the changing of mutual relationships.

§ **159.** Imitations are primarily repetitions. They are different from the repetitions of homophonic composition in that they do not occur in the same voice and often differ in the time interval they allow to elapse before entering.

§ **160.** The term imitation is of course metaphorical. When the second voice repeats a unit or a phrase—i.e. the tones and rhythms—of the first voice, it gives the impression that it desires to 'imitate' the first voice. As a rule the second voice should begin its imitation in such a manner that at least a considerable part of it sounds together with the pattern it imitates, as its accompaniment.

§ **161.** Imitations can be:
(*a*) Strict, repeating every tone and interval in the same rhythm. These may either begin on the same tone in the same or in another octave, or be transposed and begin on a different tone, and, if necessary, use substitute tones to preserve the proper intervallic relations.

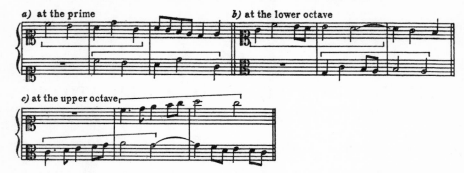

Augmentations, diminutions and inversions can also be strict if they preserve the proportions of the original.

(b) Semi-strict, repeating only the rhythm exactly. These do not begin on the same tone as the original; and so in many cases they require the use of substitute tones to repeat the true size of an interval, whether it be major or minor (2s, 7s, 3s or 6s), or perfect or diminished (5s or 4s), etc.

In the following examples the symbols (+) and (−) mark the major and minor intervals respectively. Occasionally, as in (e), (f) and (g), strict imitations are possible, but in most cases semi-strict imitations occur, with major intervals answering minor ones, and vice-versa.

(c) Free, changing intervals and sometimes the rhythm too. These are of no use in strict counterpoint.

(d) In augmentation. These are produced by multiplying the length of every note or rest by the same number. If, for instance, the augmentation were to double the original pattern, then for every half note a whole note would be used; and for every quarter note a half note, and for every dotted quarter note a dotted half note, etc. If the multiplying figure were three, the half note would be answered by a dotted whole note, etc.; and if it were four, a half note would be answered by a double whole note, etc.

(e) In diminution. These proceed in a similar manner, dividing rhythms by two, three, four, etc. If the original is halved, every whole note is answered by a half note, every half note by a quarter note, every dotted quarter note by a dotted eighth note, etc. It will not always be possible to make a graphic presentation of dividing by three.

(f) Inverted, preserving the rhythm or its proportions exactly, but answering every interval in the opposite direction. Inversions which preserve the size of the intervals exactly can be obtained if the tonic of a tonality is answered by the third (as in (a)). If this is done, all intervals will be answered by the same-sized intervals.

Inversion can be combined with either augmentation or diminution, as shown in the following example:

§ 162. In some circumstances it is possible to produce true imitation by answering the tonic with the dominant, as in (a) and (b) below; this happens in fugue writing. It is sometimes done with other intervals as well, as in (c) and (d):

§ **163.** Imitations which begin on a tone other than the initial tone of the original phrase and preserve the strict intervallic relationships by means of substitute tones, can be used to produce modulations.

CADENCES WITH IMITATIONS IN TWO VOICES

§ **164.** Ex. 82 includes imitations at various intervals, the imitating patterns being one or two measures long. The examples end with cadences that either move to the tonic or bring about modulations to other degrees. Notice the difference between imitations in lower and upper voices—which is that they produce different harmonies. Also notice that when the imitation enters, the first voice accompanies it with considerable rhythmic change. As mentioned before, it is advisable for a voice to move in smaller notes when the second voice has long notes. Suspensions can be used to advantage in such situations, too.

Ex. 82 (cont.)

IMITATIONS IN INVERSION, AUGMENTATION AND DIMINUTION

§ 165. In Ex. 83 the imitations are in inversion. In Ex. 84 the second voice appears in augmentation. In such cases it sometimes happens that the augmenting voice begins simultaneously with the pattern, as in 84c. In Ex. 85 augmentation is combined with inversion. In Ex. 86 diminution is illustrated; it is combined with inversion in 86d.

Ex. 83

Ex. 83 (cont.)

§ 166. Combinations of augmentation or diminution and inversion belong to the more complicated forms of counterpoint which only appear in compositions and need not be stressed in a textbook. It should be mentioned, however, that changes in the answering interval, and even of tonality too, can be found in masterpieces. Some of the most complicated imitations, in the form of canons, are used by Bach in his *Musical Offering*, where he writes, among other things, long canons in which one of the voices or more moves in retrograde motion—that is, it starts with the last tone and moves in the opposite direction to the first tone.

IMITATIONS IN THREE VOICES

§ 167. In Ex. 87 imitations in three voices are given. In these examples it is not just the initial pattern (marked (*a*)) that is imitated, but, within the course of the example, other fragments (marked (*b*) and (*c*)) are imitated also. It can be considered a rule, almost, that the imitation should begin before the original pattern ends. In 87*a* the third voice only enters after the end of the first voice's pattern, but it is still before the end of the imitation in the second voice. In this respect 87*b* is a better example.

Ex. 87 Modulations with Imitations

§ **168.** Working out all of these possibilities is quite useful in itself, but it will only be really worth while if the ability to write quickly, correctly and fluently is achieved. These are *preliminary exercises*, and their value will be realized in the writing of contrapuntal compositions. It might be too late to make use of them only then. It is further recommended that all the examples should be read and played, and the attempt made to recognize that these short exercises develop coherence and logic, and to realize the great number of possibilities in approaching a contrapuntally elaborate style. It pays at times to begin an otherwise simple example with one of these imitations, or to use some of them during the course of an example.

X

SEVENTH COMPOSITIONAL APPLICATION: CANONS IN TWO AND THREE VOICES

GENERAL CONSIDERATIONS

§ **169.** If one voice or more continuously imitates another voice using the same intervals as that voice, and persists in this throughout the whole of a piece (except perhaps for a small cadential segment), a *canon* is produced. An infinite or perpetual canon does not provide an ending to the imitation but, on the contrary, arranges the last measures so that they fit onto the first measures. At certain places in these canons, then, one finds repetition marks.

§ **170.** Brahms demanded that canons should be strict, i.e. that the intervals with which they begin should remain the same throughout the whole imitation and that the exact rhythm should be preserved also. In free composition it sometimes happens that a part of the imitation changes the rhythm; this may be excused on account of certain other advantages, but it has no application in our exercises. Nevertheless, in 89*a* and *b* imitations are presented which change several times from augmentation to diminution and vice versa. Taking into account that features of the rhythm are even more conspicuous than features of the intervals, one must doubt whether such an imitation fulfils the main purpose of this technique, i.e. to produce a perceptible coherence between the voices.

§ **171.** Canons at intervals other than primes, 8s or 5s are not always easily produced, especially as one must, in a correct canon, answer every interval not only according to its general description (3, 4, 5, etc.), but also according to its exact size (it may be major, minor, diminished, etc.). Beginning at the third, fourth or sixth would force one either to use substitute tones, or to avoid such tones as require substitutes from the start.

COMMENT ON CANONS, EXS. 88–90

Canons at the prime will sound better when performed by voices of different colour than when played on the piano. On the piano, of course, the crossing of voices obscures their meaning, as in 88*a*. In this respect 88*b* is much more satisfactory because the second voice enters at the octave. The next canon, at the lower fifth (88c), is built as a perpetual canon. The answer at the lower fifth cannot entirely avoid subdominant characteristics. Thus the f in ms. 7 is answered by bb; in the same measure, and also in ms. 8, f♯ is used, but in spite of this the bb in the tenor in ms. 8 seems a little remote. The repetition of the bb in the cadential segment at mss. 11 and 12 sounds smoother.

In 88d no substitute is necessary because the leading voice avoids the tone b, and so possesses a neutral rather than a subdominant character.

In attempting to write canons in the modes like those in 88e–h, one must either renounce true repetition of the intervals or use substitutes which would change the nature of the mode in question. It is one of the advantages of major and minor that their tonality can be preserved in spite of deviations by substitute tones.

In 89a and b the intervals are answered strictly, but the imitating voice changes from augmentation to diminution, and vice versa. Such an exercise is not of much value to beginners. However, similar things were customary in contrapuntal epochs. Mirror canons and enigmatic canons were produced, and it became a habit among musicians to offer one another the task of finding the clue to a canon when it was given in only one voice, there being no indication as to where the second, third or fourth voices would enter, or whether they were in augmentation, inversion, etc. Even Brahms entertained his friends in this manner during their excursions into the forests of Vienna.

These two canons, and also the three-voice canon in Ex. 90, are perpetual canons. The three-voice canon of Ex. 90 tries imitation at intervals which produce unnecessary difficulties. It is given here as a warning as to what a beginner should attempt. If he wants to try three-voice canons he should do it at the prime or the octave instead, or else use the upper or lower fifth in the second voice, and try to avoid the 7th and 4th tones respectively. Notice that in this example the intervals are preserved only according to their general description but not according to their exact size.

Ex. 88 Canons
a) at the prime

Ex. 88 (cont.)

e) Dorian at the upper third

f) Phrygian at the lower fourth

g) Mixolydian at the lower fourth

h) Lydian at the upper fourth

PART III
SIMPLE COUNTERPOINT IN FOUR VOICES

I

FIRST SPECIES

Cantus firmus *and whole notes in all voices*

ADVICE AND DIRECTIONS

§ 172. It is, of course, a little more difficult to write in four voices than in three, especially if one is aiming for a satisfactory fluency. It is clear that one or two tones will have to be doubled; decisions, however, as to which tones should be doubled, merely derive from interest in the best voice leading. Many theorists of harmony forbid the doubling of the third. Right or wrong in harmony, such a restriction is of no concern in counterpoint.

§ 173. Full triads should be aimed for as much as possible, provided that this does not detract from the melodic quality of the voices.

§ 174. Writing in four voices offers one more excuse for hidden parallels, i.e. that they occur between two middle voices. Hidden 5s between a middle voice and an outer voice have already been tolerated in three-voice writing. Several examples of hidden parallels will be found in Ex. 91.

§ 175. The penultimate harmony should again produce an authentic cadence, i.e. it should precede the I with a V, preferably in root position, or with the 6-chord of VII. The plagal cadence, that is IV–I, or II–I, is of no value.

§ 176. According to the rules of traditional counterpoint, if the last triad cannot be complete the third should be omitted rather than the fifth. This can be disregarded as a mere stylistic rule without technical value.

§ **177.** The student is recommended to make a few examples by adding a fourth voice to a good three-part counterpoint, as in Ex. 91, first of all. In Exs. 92 and 93 the CF appears successively in each of the voices.

COMMENT ON EXAMPLES IN FIRST SPECIES, EXS. 92 AND 93

In 92*a* the CF has been changed in the alternative example after ms. 8 so that the ending with the 6-chord of VII can be shown.

A succession of 6-chords, as in mss. 5–6 of 92*b*, often presents one with the problem of avoiding wrong parallels. Similar difficulties arise where two consecutive degrees, such as III–II in mss. 2–3 and 8–9 of 92*c*, have to be connected. Although the use of 6-chords generally helps to produce a good bass melody, the six 6-chords in 92*e* are rather excessive.

In 92*d* the threefold repetition of *e* in the highest voice is very monotonous.

It was not absolutely necessary to write an incomplete tonic triad in the first measure of 92*e*; however, the second measure corrects this shortcoming.

All of these examples in first species show one weakness or another. See, for example, the monotonous bass in the last three measures of 92*f* which could, of course, be easily corrected. The same is true of 92*g*. In 92*h* the return of the bass to *c* in ms. 5 sounds weak. In 92*i* the succession of three tones, *g–e♭–f*, in mss. 3–5 of the soprano is repeated in mss. 8–10, making it a poor CF. It does not help that, when repeated, the three tones are harmonized differently. The shortcomings of the two outer voices do more harm than their merits can overcome. The descending line of the CF in the last three measures of 92*k* is treated better than the same line in 92*j*.

The examples in minor (Ex. 93) not only have the same defects as the preceding examples in major, but they also suffer from the requirements of neutralization. These difficulties will be lessened only when the restrictions caused by neutralization are loosened a little and richer movement becomes possible. Even though any hope of producing faultless examples in minor is slight at the moment, it pays to try doing them because one becomes acquainted with some of the difficulties they offer.

Of the minor examples, 93*b* and *c* are better than 93*a*. As a result of an effort to use the ascending scale in the CF, 93*d* is forced into several shortcomings.

One of the reasons for the dullness of these examples is that the endings of most CFs admit of no other harmonies than I–V–I in root position. Another reason is that they resemble too closely simple harmony examples where the voices move only as much as is required by the need for harmonic progression. But at the same time the harmonic progressions are not as powerful as those which one would select for a good harmony example.

Ex. 91

a) (from 52*f*)

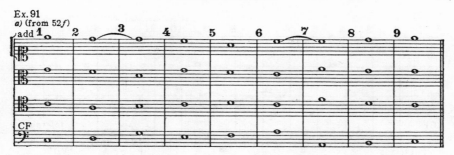

b) (from 52*g*)

c) (Minor: from 53*a*)

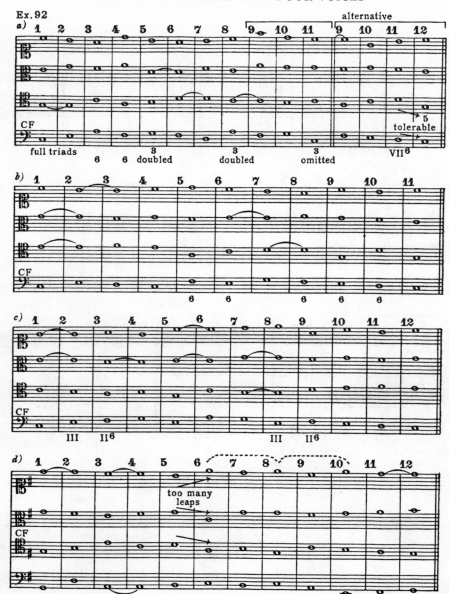

Ex. 92 (cont.)

e) the same

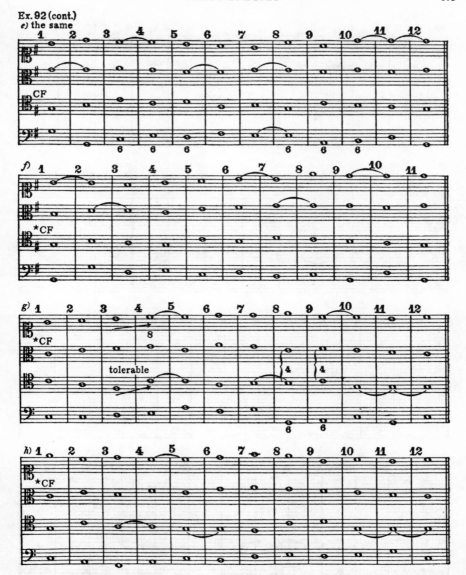

f)

g)

tolerable

h)

* CF by Bellermann

Ex. 92 (cont.)

II

SECOND SPECIES

Half notes in one or two voices to a cantus firmus

ADVICE AND DIRECTIONS

§ 178. There are no new rules for this species. Once again one must be careful over passing notes. There is not so much scope for writing half notes in two voices as there is for writing them in one, and so one is sometimes forced to interrupt their movement. Accordingly, one should not even attempt half notes in three voices in these examples.

COMMENT ON EXAMPLES IN SECOND SPECIES, EXS. 94 AND 95

The hidden 5s between the outer voices in ms. 10 of 94a are difficult to avoid. The repetition of the interval of a fourth in mss. 2 and 4 produces a kind of sequential phrasing, and this should be avoided.

In 94b there are two interesting passing notes, in mss. 2 and 4. Both produce dissonances which would be considered rough in a lesser number of voices.

A syncopation is probably the only solution at ⊗ in ms. 9 of 94c. There is a certain stiffness in the melody of this example; after four ascending notes (mss. 5–6) the tenor should not then make a leap in the same direction. Notice also the intermittent and hidden 5s.

The bass in 94d is extremely stiff. And the meeting of the three upper voices on the note d in ms. 7 is very poor. The parallel 5s could have been avoided; thus the tenor might have gone to g in ms. 7, for instance. It is not wrong to use half notes occasionally in one of the voices, as for instance in the cadential segment in ms. 10 (⊗).

The repetitions of c in 94e are awkward, the more so as the tone c is always part of a chord on F or C (II). But ms. 10 takes advantage of the fact that there are two possibilities for completing the incomplete harmony of the three lower voices, with its d and c in the soprano.

Ms. 11 of 94f sounds weak because the diminished triad of VII appears on the first half note—before the V; although it is a substitute for V, it is not a good companion for it. The leap of an 8 in the bass in ms. 7 (at ⊕) is unavoidable because no passing note whether it moved upwards or downwards would lead into a consonance with the CF's a (alto) in ms. 8.

The ending of the tenor in ms. 10 of 94g is very good. Otherwise, the bass line should not move so much in broken chord form (mss. 2–6). However, it is often difficult to avoid this, and though it is not highly artistic, it is not wrong. There is no objection to an occasional syncopation as in mss. 9–10 of 94i. In ms. 11 there occurs again the connecting of VII and V. In this example it would only be possible to find a better solution if in mss. 10 and 11 at least one other voice employed half notes.

There are not many advantages in using half notes in two voices as in 94j and k. In most cases they accomplish little more than the completion of triads. There is not much chance for the use of passing notes (marked + in these examples), and even cadential measures do not profit much. Already the strict movement of one voice in notes of the same length is producing some stiffness; if half notes are used in more than one voice this tendency increases.

In 95b the crossing of alto and tenor in the last measure is unavoidable because of the low position of the CF. In many of these examples the introduction of the leading tone is accomplished through suspension (marked ✳). All cross-related tones are properly neutralized (*neutr.*).

In 95c the simultaneous syncopation of alto and tenor produces a 6/5 chord on a. The tenor in 95d has to return to b♭ in ms. 6 to be neutralized; the soprano then crosses the alto by leaping an octave. The only other second half note possible in the soprano is g, which would make the leap a sixth. This would be possible as it would not produce hidden parallels.

In 95e, ms. 4, it is impossible to neutralize the a♭ in the tenor. It is neutralized, however, an octave higher in the alto.

There are a number of shortcomings in 95h. The reason is that the a in the alto in ms. 4 was sustained when it should not have been; this forced the soprano to cross the alto and produce an even worse continuation. The repetition of a tone in ms. 6 (∧) is very poor, but not entirely impossible. Such an example should be altered throughout.

95j is a very poor example as the tone a appears three times in the tenor like the afterbeating note of an Alberti bass. In ms. 7 of 95k the augmented triad is interesting for it appears in the form of a suspension (at ✳). The b♭ of the soprano in ms. 3 of 95l is not neutralized (⊕). This is doubtlessly the reason why the b♮ in ms. 7 is so conspicuous.

Ex.94

*).This CF and many others in this treatise are stiff, but they have been constructed so as to produce difficulties.

Ex.94(cont.)

Ex.95 Minor

Ex. 95 (cont.)

Ex. 95 (cont.)

III

THIRD SPECIES

Cantus firmus *and quarter notes*

ADVICE AND DIRECTIONS

§ **179.** Writing quarter notes in more than one voice at a time would reduce the rhythmic independence of the voices to an even greater degree than writing half notes in more than one voice did. But in addition the voices might suffer melodically from such regularity, since the only choice it would leave one would be that between passing notes and harmony notes. Instead, one might write one voice in half notes and use an occasional syncopation, a procedure which would better satisfy the requirements of counterpoint—of which the most important is the achievement of as much rhythmic differentiation as possible.

§ **180.** Stopping the half-note movement periodically is not as dangerous as in previous species because the quarter notes keep up the necessary motion. It might even be admissible to stop the half-note movement in one voice and continue it in another. One could, in this manner, gradually approach the desired goal, which is that every voice should differ rhythmically from every other voice.

§ **181.** In the following examples in third species the CF is placed in each of the voices in turn, the quarter notes being sometimes above and sometimes below the CF. It makes a difference, then, where the added whole notes are placed. There are too many possibilities here for us to be able to consider them all.

COMMENT ON EXAMPLES IN THIRD SPECIES, EXS. 96 AND 97

In ms. 3 of 96*a* the *c*♯ in the bass is fortunately not doubled; this permits the bass to use *g*♯ (at ⊕), which otherwise would have produced a 6/4-chord. The cambiata always offers opportunities, as shown by the three instances in this example, but the one in mss. 4–5 is questionable as it contains three dissonances in succession, the last one being a fourth.

The leap of a fourth, as in mss. 5 and 7 of 96*b*, is often very useful for keeping up the movement. The ending of 96*b* had better not be permitted at the moment as in ms. 11 the alto makes an unexplained dissonance (7) with both the soprano and the tenor. An alternative ending is given; this, though correct, suffers from unsatisfactory positioning in the tenor.

The alternative for mss. 3 and 4 of 96c shows that the tritone can be avoided. In this example there is not perhaps enough change in harmony.

96d is also very stiff. The tone c, which appears three times in the CF (bass), offers certain difficulties because the harmony above it can only be IV or II; VII is excluded. If one takes into consideration the fact that e appears twice, too (once as a IV), the dullness of the harmony becomes understandable.

In 96e and f half notes and some syncopations are added. The voice in half notes often has to use leaps where stepwise motion would be preferable, in order to keep the quarter-note voice fluent.

In 97a there twice appear two dissonances in succession—in mss. 1 and 11. These can be tolerated. This example is less monotonous than one would expect on looking at the alto from mss. 7 to 10. Whether the lack of neutralization in ms. 6 of the alto (at ⊕) can be excused because the a and g appear so often, is questionable—at least if we follow the rules. But it is difficult to say how one could have avoided the leap of the soprano in half notes in ms. 10: f and f♯ cannot be used, and as the two middle voices both move in contrary motion to the b, only the d can be doubled. Unfortunately the soprano is not in the right position for doing even this.

In 97b, ms. 4, the b♭ is not neutralized in the alto (at ⊕). It would have been extremely difficult to neutralize it without changing the tenor entirely. Whether the shifting of the b♭ to the tenor in ms. 6 and its neutralization there in ms. 8 solves this problem is questionable. Two half notes have to be used in the bass in ms. 6, too, to neutralize its b♭.

In 97c the cambiata in mss. 7–8 is perhaps an excuse for the appearance of a descending scale so near the end. The passing note g in ms. 8 of the tenor (⊕) is dissonant to the f♯ in both soprano and bass; the seventh to the soprano is then followed by another seventh, f♯-e, which would not have occurred if the soprano had remained a whole note, f♯.

In 97d, ms. 5, the passing note a♭ in the tenor (at ⊕) offers practically the only opportunity for neutralization; this is because there is no other place where the a♭ can go down to g without causing parallel 5s. In ms. 10 the cambiata provides an acceptable excuse for the appearance of the tone e♭ on the second beat.

The quarter notes in the bass of 97e traverse rather a large compass, but they have to descend after the climax in ms. 5 in order to neutralize certain tones (those at ✕). An alternative in quarter notes is provided for the tenor in mss. 7–8.

In 97f the movement in half notes could not easily be continued throughout without interruption. In ms. 7 it would have been impossible to find a substitute for the e♭ in the alto that doubles the suspension in the soprano (at ⊕).

The descending passage in ms. 6 of 97g is necessary because of the unneutralized a♮ (X) in ms. 5. This makes intermittent 8s between soprano and bass almost unavoidable; the solution shown in the alternative avoids them but is poor.

The incorrect cambiata in 97h, mss. 2–3, is psychologically interesting. It shows that a formula sanctified by convention can be satisfactory even if it does not obey all the rules. In addition it provides an interesting escape from the snare of the turning-points. The alternatives for mss. 2–3 take advantage of the possibility of movement to the tone e♮ onto which the suspension should resolve. This is permissible.

Ex. 96

Ex. 96 (cont.)

Ex. 97 Minor

Ex. 97 (cont.)

IV

FOURTH SPECIES

Syncopations in one voice to a cantus firmus *with* (1) *whole notes, and* (2) *half notes and quarter notes in the remaining voices*

ADVICE AND DIRECTIONS

§ **182.** There are no new rules for the writing of syncopations in four voices. One must not, however, forget the warning about anticipating the tone of resolution in a voice above a suspension ('bad' seventh). The rules of strict counterpoint only permit such anticipation in the lowest voice, but this can be extended to apply to any voice below the suspension.

§ **183.** Of the examples that follow, Ex. 98 presents whole notes in the two remaining voices, and Ex. 99 half notes in one and quarter notes in the other. In Ex. 100 both the latter types of note are found in the minor tonality. Suspensions are marked *S* in all of the examples. In the writing of syncopations with both half notes and quarter notes the voice which usually offers the most difficulty is the one in half notes. Broken chords and other kinds of unmelodic movement are often unavoidable in this voice. In minor the difficulties are increased by the need for neutralization.

COMMENT ON EXAMPLES IN FOURTH SPECIES, EXS. 98–100

In 98*a* one can see how often the voices in whole notes do not make up complete triads—they do not do this in mss. 2, 3, 4, 7, 8, 9 and 11. In ms. 5, on the other hand, there appears a fully-fledged 6/5-chord (at ⊗), the result of the suspension of both the alto and the tenor below the soprano; the syncopation in the bass which is treated as a consonance, moves upward, the resolution coming on the second half note. In ms. 12 there is perhaps no choice but to have two harmonies, II–V, with both the alto and tenor moving in half notes, since the only tone common to mss. 11 and 12 is *a*, the root of a diminished triad, which cannot be used in the bass.

In 99*a* it is not very good beginning the soprano syncopations with an octave to the bass note on the third beat. Some difficulties are caused in this example by the CF in the tenor which is in part too low and in part too high. It would have been better if it had not extended over such a large range.

Certain difficulties are caused by the strict application of neutralization in the examples in minor. In 100*a* the appearance of the unneutralized *b♭* in ms. 6 of the tenor makes it necessary for the tenor to return to *b♭* in ms. 10 against a suspension (*c*) in the soprano. The tenor then has to use quarter notes to bring about neutralization before the soprano resolves its suspension on to *b♮* on the third beat. In 100*b* the neutralization in the soprano in mss. 7 and 8 is brought about indirectly. In 100*c* the *d* in the alto in ms. 4 is neutralized in the tenor with which it is a prime. The *d* in ms. 5 of the soprano (at X), however, is still not properly neutralized. In this latter example notice also the double suspension in the alto and bass in ms. 8 which produces a II4/3-chord.[1]

_____
[1] Comment in this paragraph is by the editor.

Ex. 99

V

FIFTH SPECIES[1]

Mixed notes in one or more voices to a cantus firmus, *with whole notes, half notes, quarter notes or syncopations in the remaining voices*

ADVICE AND DIRECTIONS

§ **184.** In Ex. 101 five variants of fifth species are presented. The voice in mixed notes and CF apart, 101*a* contains whole notes in both added voices, 101*b* whole notes in the one and half notes in the other, 101*c* half notes in both added voices, and 101*d* half notes in one and syncopations in the other; 101*e* has mixed notes in all the voices except the CF. Only three examples in major and two in minor are given although many more variants are possible; they should all be practised systematically. There are no new rules for this species to add to those mentioned for writing in three voices (see §§ 133 ff.).

COMMENT ON EXAMPLES IN FIFTH SPECIES, EX. 101

There are some shortcomings in 101*b*, in particular the broken chord in the tenor (mss. 1–2) and the repetitions in the bass (ms. 3 and mss. 5–6). In 101*c* the difficulty of obtaining a fluent ending necessitates a change from half note to quarter note movement in the soprano in ms. 10.

101*d* is an especially difficult example involving four different species, and it is not entirely satisfactory. The alto in particular suffers from excessive repetition and limited range. Two deviations from usual practice in this example should be mentioned: the appearance of a passing note on the first strong beat in ms. 9 of the tenor—the result of continuing the descending scale line—and the syncopations in all three added voices in ms. 10, made necessary by the syncopated *f*♯ in the bass which could only produce a 6/5-chord with the voices above it. Actually it is much easier to achieve satisfactory results with all voices in mixed notes, as in 101*e*.

[1] Text and comment added by the editor.

Ex.101 Mixed Notes

VI

ADDITION OF VOICES[1]

The addition of one or two voices to given examples in two or three voices

ADVICE AND DIRECTIONS

§ **185.** In § 137 dealing with cadences in three voices, it was recommended that an extra third voice should be added to examples previously worked out in two voices, as a preliminary exercise. The value of this procedure was shown, and advice for the treatment of added voices was given, in the subsequent sections (§ 138 to § 141), and the procedure was illustrated in Exs. 69, 70 and 71.

§ **186.** In Ex. 102 fourth voices are added in a similar manner to examples previously written in three voices. Some of the examples are selected from the sections on the various species; others from those on modulations without CF.

§ **187.** In Ex. 103 two voices are added to examples originally constructed as cadences in two voices (Ex. 40).

§ **188.** Finally, Exs. 104–7 illustrate how first one and then two voices are added to modulations in two given voices.[2] With reference to these latter examples the author has appended the following explanation:

Many of the modulations are not as good as they might be since they are intended wholly as models for the student. The rules, here applied for pedagogical purposes, are so strict as to limit the possibilities, so that perfect solutions almost become mere hazards—at least for the teacher who should observe everything he asks from the student. The latter should of course avoid major faults, and his minor errors and other shortcomings should be corrected by the teacher not with the aim of making his examples perfect, but simply to show him what can help in special cases. In adding third and fourth voices the student is allowed to change the cadence of an example composed for two voices, especially when it has a certain characteristic 'fundamental

---

[1] Text and comment added by the editor.
[2] These examples were not included in the original text but were found among other examples written by Schoenberg for his counterpoint classes. They are included here by the editor as being especially pertinent to both problems in the addition of voices and problems of modulation to the various regions.

bass-line' and a lower voice has to be added. Sometimes one cannot avoid the crossing of voices, especially when observing the turning-points and neutralizing cross-related tones.

COMMENT ON EXAMPLES WITH ADDED VOICES, EXS. 102–7

The endings of some of the given voices—alto in 102c, tenor in 102g, tenor in 103b —are slightly changed to allow more flexibility in the added voices and also to make it easier to avoid wrong parallels. The crossing of voices that occurs in some of the examples—it is marked by arrows in 102f, g, and h, 103b, and 104e—is often the result of a large compass being traversed by one of the given voices. In some instances an octave leap in one voice restores the voices to their original positions (see alto in 102f, ms. 8, soprano in 102h, ms. 4, and alto in 103b, ms. 4).

102g and h present modulations to the *submediant* and *subtonic* regions respectively. As both examples are without CF, it might be wise to review cadences and modulation in three voices both with and without CF before attempting this kind of exercise. See §§ 144 ff. in particular. In general the procedure is the same as that for three voices, special care being necessary in the bringing about of neutralization in the added voice.

The high note in the alto—itself an added voice in 75f—at the beginning of 102h forces the soprano into an unusually high register. This situation might be rectified by placing the first measure of the alto an octave lower than it is in the original, as shown in the two alternatives.

Somewhat unusual treatment of the cambiata takes place in both 102h, ms. 2, and 103a, ms. 3. In the former instance the cambiata ends on a weak beat; and it is further suspect as 8s with the voice below it are produced at the beginning and end. In the latter, the cambiata appears in a more acceptable form, beginning and ending on strong beats, but it uses eighth notes instead of the usual quarter notes.

In the modulatory examples, Exs. 104–7, there are places where it appears that the treatment of the dissonance departs from the practice followed up to this point. For example, in 104a, ms. 1, the f♯ on the fourth beat in the bass produces a seventh with the tenor, which is certainly not the usual way of 'suspending' this upper tone, although it may be said to be 'prepared' on the third beat of the measure and to 'resolve' on the first beat of the next measure—a process akin to the treatment of seventh-chords in harmony. The suspension in the alto in ms. 3 (at ⊗) also occurs in a somewhat unusual position, appearing on the second and weak beat rather than on the usual strong beat. The suspension in the tenor in ms. 5 (S) is only unusual in that the dissonance is brought about on the second half of the second beat by the d in the bass, and that the resolution, which occurs on the fourth beat after an interruption, in turn produces a suspension in the bass. Finally, notice the unusual cambiata beginning on the second beat in ms. 2 of this example.

In 104*b* the 6/4-chord in the cadence in ms. 5 is treated as a double suspension in the soprano and alto and resolved accordingly. The *a* in the alto on the third beat, however, does not seem to have been prepared as a dissonance (fourth) to the tenor; it would have been if it had appeared on the second beat instead (as in the alternative). The explanation of this unprepared tone which is perhaps most nearly compatible with our rules, is that it is part of a cambiata-like figure beginning on the second beat.

There are two passing notes in succession (they are marked + +), in scale-lines in 104*c*, ms. 4, 106*a*, ms. 5, and 106*c*, ms. 2. Such dissonances are especially interesting when used in conjunction with another dissonance, like the 4/2-suspension in the tenor in 106*a*; here the tenor resolves against the second of two passing notes in the alto which are also dissonant to the soprano. The harsh effect produced by allowing dissonances to appear on two, or even three, consecutive notes, may often be alleviated by changing the movement in one of the voices, as shown in 104*e*, ms. 4 (at ⊗). In 106*c* the *c*♯ in the bass and the *e* in the tenor (at ☐) are dissonant to the *d*♮ in the soprano on the fourth beat of ms. 3; this would best be explained as an anticipation of the suspension which occurs on the first beat of the next measure, its normal position. Finally, with regard to rather unusual treatment of the dissonance, mention should be made of the roundabout interrupted resolution in 107*b*, ms. 2 (at ⊗); there are two intervening tones here before the resolution is reached.

Although neutralization is handled carefully in all of these examples, as the author has often mentioned, it frequently presents difficulties that are almost impossible to overcome. In ms. 1 of 106*c*, for example, the attempt to express as many characteristics of the *tonic* region, *C* major, as possible in only three beats, has prevented neutralization of the *c* in the bass (✗). However, this note does appear at the same time in both the tenor and the soprano with proper neutralization.

In 107*b* the bass line undoubtedly contains too many leaps in mss. 3 and 4; at least, there are more of them than was usual in the preceding examples. The simultaneous leaps in ms. 3 of 107*c* by tenor and bass are not recommended by the author who prefers instead to change the rhythm in the tenor (as in brackets) and allow the two voices to cross momentarily.

Ex.102 Addition of a Fourth Voice to Examples in Three Voices

Ex. 102 (cont.)
e) (from 68*a*)

Ex. 102 (cont.)

g) Modulation: F-d (from 74*a*)

h) Modulation: a-G (from 75*f*)

alternative I

alternative II

* treble clef is used because of
  the high register.

Ex.103 Addition of Two Voices to Two Given Voices

a) (from 40*a*)

b) (from 40*k*)

Ex. 104 Third and Fourth Voices Added to Two Voices: **to submediant**

* Bracket indicates added voices

Ex. 107 to Subtonic (a-G)

VII

EIGHTH COMPOSITIONAL APPLICATION:[1] CADENCES, MODULATIONS AND INTER-MEDIARY REGIONS WITHOUT ADDED VOICES

ADVICE AND DIRECTIONS

§ 189. The examples in this chapter present cadences and modulations in four voices without either CF or added voices. An initial cadence is given—one in major in 108*a* and one in minor in 109*a*—and then many alternative cadences containing different continuations are added. The examples illustrate (1) cadences—108*a* and *b*, 109*a* and *b*; (2) cadences with intermediary regions—108*c* and *d*, 109*c* and *d*; (3) modulations to various regions—108*e*, *g*, *h* and *j*, 109*e*, *f*, *g* and *j*; (4) modulations with intermediary regions—108*f*, *i* and *k*, 109*h* and *i*.

§ 190. As the advice relating to the above categories in three voices applies to four-voice writing as well, it might be advisable to start by reviewing the following sections in Simple Counterpoint in Three Voices: Chapter VI, Cadences Without Cantus Firmus (§§ 135 ff.); Chapter VII, Cadences to Various Regions and Modulation (§§ 144 ff.); and Chapter VIII, Intermediary Regions (§§ 148 ff.). The sections on cadences and modulations in two voices might also be reviewed, special attention being paid to the concepts of region and neutralization (see § 92 and § 96 in particular).

COMMENT ON CADENCES AND MODULATIONS IN FOUR VOICES, EXS. 108 AND 109

In the examples that follow it will be noticed that a complete harmony is obtained on nearly every beat. This is not necessarily to be aimed at in four-voice writing, but it is nearly always the result of real independent movement in four or more voices. In addition many seventh-chords and seventh-chord inversions are produced; they are usually brought about by passing notes (marked (7)) or—and this is more interesting—by suspensions (S). Notice especially the 6/5-chord suspensions—in 108*f*,

---

[1] Text and comment added by the editor.

j (where the suspension occurs twice in succession), and *k* (it is actually the result of the passing *d*♯ in the soprano here), and in 109*g* (it comes twice in ms. 3), *i* and *j*. The 6/4-chord also appears under similar circumstances—most commonly as a suspension in the cadence, as in 108*a*, *g* and *k*, and 109*e*. In 108*k* what seems to be a resolution into a 6/4-chord in ms. 4 of the soprano, is better considered as part of a cambiata. Two interesting 4/2-chords—suspensions in the bass—appear in 109*a* and *i*.

With so much movement in all voices it is not unusual to find frequent instances of consecutive dissonances in different voices, occurring either as combinations of passing notes (108*c*, *f* and *k*, and 109*a*—at ⊗—where it is especially striking) or as suspensions with passing notes (108*b*, *f*, *h* and *j*; 109*c*, *d*, *h* and *j*). In 108*h*, ms. 4, the resolution of the suspension in the alto occurs simultaneously with a passing dissonance in the tenor. In 108*j*, ms. 3, both the soprano and tenor pass while the suspension is being held in the alto. Probably the most interesting combination of dissonances takes place in 109*c*, ms. 2, where the alto moves to a preparation on the second half of the first beat (quite irregularly, it must be noted, as it is a diminished fifth above the bass) while the soprano is still suspended, then resolves in its turn on the second half of the second beat against another suspension in the soprano. A succession of overlapping suspensions involving the upper three voices then occurs, and it continues clear into the beginning of the next measure.

In modulations to and from the various regions, whether they end in the original tonic region or not, neutralization of the cross-related tones is carried out very carefully. Usually a very strong cadence containing elements of the subdominant (IV and II) as well as the dominant, confirms the final region. The dominant is further stressed by the frequent use of I 6/4. Deceptive progressions (V–VI) are used in several places, not only to extend cadences, as in 108*d*, but also to make possible more transitory movement through intermediary regions, as in 108*f* and 109*h*.

Ex.108 Cadences and Modulations

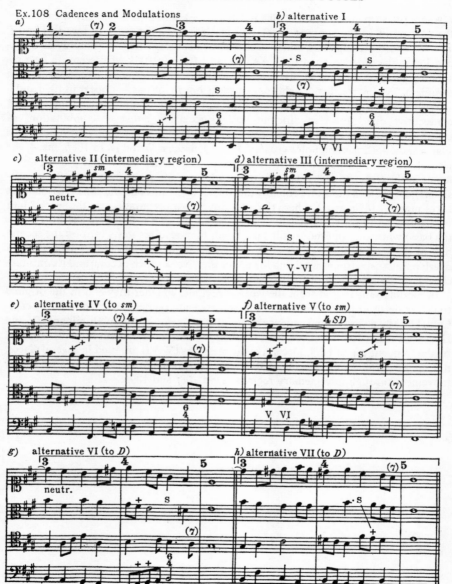

Ex.108 (cont.)

i) alternative VIII (to D)   j) alternative IX (to m)

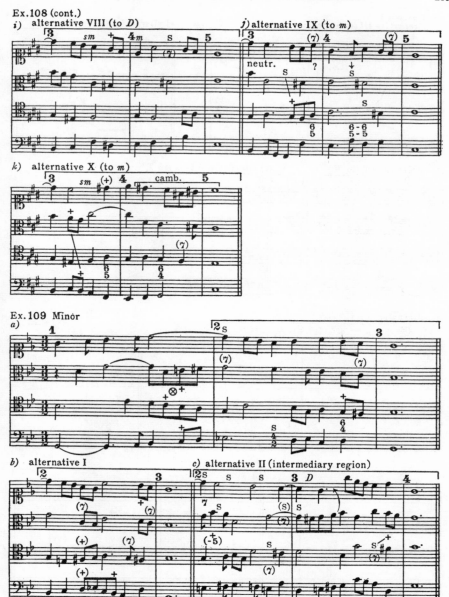

k) alternative X (to m)

Ex.109 Minor
a)

b) alternative I   c) alternative II (intermediary region)

Ex.109 (cont.)

VIII

NINTH COMPOSITIONAL APPLICATION:[1]
IMITATION IN FOUR VOICES

ADVICE AND DIRECTIONS

§ **191.** Imitations of various sorts in two and three voices have already been considered in Chapter IX of Simple Counterpoint in Three Voices (§§ 157 ff.). It would be advisable for the student to review this entire chapter, paying special attention to Ex. 87 which illustrates imitations in three voices, before proceeding to imitations in four voices.

§ **192.** As with the above examples, the examples in four voices that follow (Exs. 110 and 111) introduce imitations not only at the beginning but also at all points during the course of examples. Most of the imitations (marked with brackets) are strict; there are a few cases of inversion, diminution, and augmentation, and slight variants are also introduced. All of the examples are presented as modulations to regions in major or minor.

COMMENT ON IMITATIONS IN FOUR VOICES, EXS. 110 AND 111[2]

In 110*a* the figure for imitation is introduced in the tenor against two other contrapuntal figures in the soprano and bass. The imitation in the alto overlaps the tenor figure in ms. 1. The imitation in ms. 3 of the tenor is irregular in so far as it begins on a strong rather than a weak beat. It will be noticed that the *f* in the soprano in ms. 1 (X) is unneutralized. However, as the *f♯* only appears in the third measure and the *f* is neutralized in ms. 2 of the tenor, this lapse may be overlooked.[3] The unusual 6/4-chord in the cadence (ms. 5) can only be explained under our rules if we regard the *g* in the soprano (a fourth above the bass) as a suspension that resolves indirectly onto the *f♯* at the end of the measure.

In 110*b* the unneutralized *d* of the tenor in ms. 2 (X) is neutralized by the bass in the same register, and then again in a higher register by the alto. As the *d♯* does not

---

[1] Text and comment added by the editor except where noted.

[2] These examples were not included by Schoenberg in the original text, but were written for his counterpoint classes. As they follow up the previous discussion of imitation in two or three voices so well, it seems justified including them here.

[3] The comments in this paragraph up to here were written into the examples by Schoenberg.

appear until the end of the next measure this should allow sufficient time to take care of the cross relation.[1]

The imitative figure appears five times in 110*c*, which is given two endings—they are on the mediant and the dominant respectively. The *d* in ms. 3 of the soprano ought to have been neutralized before the first ending in *e* minor, but there need be no such considerations with regard to the modulation to *G* major in the second ending. However, the late appearance of the cross-related *d♯* at the very end of ms. 4 improves the situation somewhat.[1]

The imitation in 110*f* is considerably longer and more interesting than that in the preceding examples. In ms. 2 of the bass (at ⊗) the *g♮* may seem surprising so soon after the *g♯* in the soprano. It must be remembered, however, that the *g♯* refers to the tonic region, *a* minor, and is neutralized correctly, while the *g♮* is to be considered as part of the scale of *e* minor, the five-minor region, which follows.[1] Two alternatives have been added for the second half of ms. 3 (⊠) in order to show how the broken chord in the bass may be avoided.[1]

The two examples in Ex. 111 carry out various forms of imitation in conjunction with modulation through intermediary regions. 111*a* modulates by way of the submediant region (*sm*, or *a* minor) to the region of the dominant (*D*, or *G* major), while 111*b* interposes the mediant region (*m*, or *e* minor) between the tonic and dominant regions.

These examples include imitation in inversion (*inv.*), augmentation, and diminution (*dim.*), and also rhythmic variants (*var.*).

In ms. 5 of 111*a* the soprano has a dissonant fourth with the bass on the first beat (marked ⊗). To comply with explanations of dissonances given previously in this book, it should be explained as part of a cambiata (see the dotted lines).

---

[1] The comments in these sentences were written into the examples by Schoenberg.

Ex.110 Modulations with Imitations
a) to Dominant

Ex. 110 (cont.)
(*f*) to **v-minor**

Ex.111 Intermediary Regions
a) C-a-G

b) C-e-G

APPENDIX A

(*Editor's note.*—The following prefaces were written by Schoenberg. They are presented here —exactly as he wrote them—even though they are incomplete, because they state so very well his intentions regarding the nature of *Preliminary Exercises in Counterpoint*, as well as his basic philosophy with respect to the teaching of counterpoint. The first preface was written in 1936; the second—wherein he is mainly concerned with criticizing the 'Palestrina style' as the basis for teaching counterpoint—was written much later, probably just preceding the final formulation of this book. In addition, two other prefaces, partly repetitions of the following, were begun; some of their statements have been incorporated into the text at appropriate places.)

PREFACE I

PREFACE FOR THE STUDENT[1]

Counterpoint is considered mostly as a kind of *science*, as a kind of *theory* or *aesthetics*; accordingly, one who studies it expects to learn undisputed *laws* of the musical art. This interpretation would almost have been correct in former times. When contrapuntal art was the predominant musical style of the higher kind, and teachers, theorists and aestheticians had done a meritorious work in elaborating not only exactly the laws which led one successfully the right way, but also in establishing the pedagogical method to train a beginner in a reliable manner—at this time it might have seemed impossible to imagine that there could ever come about another time when these laws would not tell everything about musical art. But there did come a time when to all appearances quite other laws began to dominate the production of music.

Already in the works of J. S. Bach many of the older laws and rules are denied. It is not only that he uses the church modes only exceptionally, preferring instead to write in modern major and minor, but, in addition, his treatment of what his predecessors considered dissonances is developed and becomes much freer. He uses seventh-chords and ninth-chords, extends the idea of passing notes and changes many other restrictions by a new concept of melodic feeling. Later, in Brahms, for example, and especially in Wagner, this change went as far as possible and the face of music changed so totally that it seemed for a time anachronistic to study counterpoint at all.

However by this attitude some bad things happened. Theories came about that were based

---

[1] Underneath this heading the author has written: 'follows a Preface for the Teacher and a Preface for the Composer'. Unfortunately it appears that neither one was ever written.

on the astonishing development of the theories of harmony, which, at their best, tried to reconcile the contrapuntal style with the homophonic-harmonic style, with the result that both of them were spoiled. Depriving harmony of the consciousness of the basic degrees, on the one hand, these theories degraded counterpoint to a mere art of part leading and of a polyphony added to a preconceived harmony, on the other hand. Consequently the real nature of the art of counterpoint was controverted.

While counterpoint is the art of using a basic motive, phrase, combination, or idea of another sort—to compose music without the use of the later developed method of variation —the fulfillment of this problem is, of course, done by means of independent parts. But it is not the greater number of parts which makes a contrapuntal work greater music than one composed of a smaller number of parts. Besides, and foremost, as many theorists of the older school state, harmony is achieved through the intelligent motion of independent parts which lend each other color and meaning by their vertical changes. According to that consideration harmony, embellished by moving parts but bound to degrees, could not, on the one hand, fulfil this task, while, on the other hand, the necessary development of harmony, which is provoked by the basic problems of moving progressions, could never be brought into accord with the demands of independent parts.

On account of all this, the theory of counterpoint will here be treated in quite a different way. It will not be considered as a theory at all, but as a method of training, and the foremost purpose of this method will be to teach the pupil so that he becomes able to use his knowledge later when he composes.

Accordingly there will be developed here not only the ability of the student in voice leading, but also his introduction to very artistic and compositional principles, so that he will be led to recognize inhowfar these principles are the same as always in art. Consequently there will be no room here for eternal laws. Knowing that the laws of counterpoint have been denied by the development of our art, there will only be given here advice in more or less strict form which will be changed corresponding to a pedagogical point of view.

Counterpoint is neither aesthetics nor theory, but a more pedagogical way of training. There can be no doubt that, after two centuries of development of homophonic forms and a very complex harmony, the musical thoughts of our time are not contrapuntal but melodic-homophonic-harmonic. There can be no doubt that we are expressing our musical feeling in a much more flexible and varying manner than what contrapuntal art asks. There can be no doubt that we will not restrict our knowledge of harmony almost to the zero point on account of the necessities of the contrapuntal method of developing a musical idea. Consequently there will be no doubt that the rules and laws of this art will not appear unchangeable any more to our mind. But where we use them we will have to realize that we do so under a different concept: our laws, restrictions, defences, warnings, and even suggestions, will have the purpose to lead the pupil from the most simple forms, stepwise, to the most complicated; and this will be the reason why, on the one hand, we will make them, but, on the other hand, we will reduce their strictness, likewise stepwise, as much until they correspond, if not to what the harmonic feeling of our time demands, at least to the harmonic feeling of, for instance, a Brahms and a Wagner.[1]

---

[1] The ending of this Preface has the following note: 'the second purpose: to develop the ear of the pupil'.

PREFACE II

To base the teaching of counterpoint on Palestrina is as stupid as to base the teaching of medicine on Aesculapius. Nothing could be more remote from contemporary ideas, structurally and ideologically, than the style of this composer. Besides, his contrapuntal technique is by no means superior to that of the Dutch composers and even does not demonstrate the more difficult problems and their solutions discovered only shortly after him. The assumption that a student who only once 'has felt the satisfaction deriving from perfection will never forget it', might not be entirely wrong. But, on the one hand, why should he try to write imperfect imitations of a style when he could feel the emanation of perfection from the works of the author better than his own scribbling? And, on the other hand, there is no greater perfection in music than in Bach! No Beethoven or Haydn, not even a Mozart who was closest to it, ever attained such perfection. But it seems that this perfection does not result in a style which a student can imitate. This perfection is one of Idea, of basic conception, not one of elaboration. This latter is only the natural consequence of the profundity of the idea, and this cannot be imitated, nor can it be taught.

APPENDIX B

(*Editor's note.* The following material was collected by Schoenberg, evidently for inclusion in succeeding volumes on counterpoint—see Editor's Foreword, p. xi.)

I.

(after including Contents of present volume)

Outline

Contrapuntal Composition

Chorale Prelude
Simple Fugues: 2 Voices
Fugues: 3 Voices
Double Counterpoint in 2 Voices, of the 8ve
Double Counterpoint of the 10th
Double Counterpoint of the 12th
Combination of Double Counterpoint in 8, 10 and 12
Fugues with 2 Subjects: 3 Voices
Multiple Counterpoint

II. *Counterpoint in Homophonic Music*[1]
(after 1750) differs from Bachian Counterpoint

1. Because of the acceptance of many 7th-chords as 'non'-dissonant; besides numerous 7th-chords using substitute tones; besides all dim.7th-chords and augmented triads.
2. Melodies used dissonant tones like consonances, e.g. 6th of I and even 7th—Lanner, J. Strauss, Schubert, Delibes, Sullivan, Schumann First Quartet.
3. In contrast to contrapuntal themes, which are not based on chords (difficult to harmonize; Bach Fugues in C major and c minor, and all others), homophonic melodies are based on chord progressions which move less fast than the melody.
4. Combination of superimposed Themes (or phrases, or motives) in homophony does not serve in the same manner as double counterpoint in 8, 10, 12, etc. See end of Meistersinger Vorspiel, or Durchführung of Schoenberg First String Quartet, or Scherzo and Trio of Schoenberg Second Quartet.
5. 'Independent' motion of accompanying voices often do not contain thematic material.

[1] Derived from another source.

6. 'Animated' subordinate voices, with or without motival features or imitations.
7. Canonic forms (or sections): Schubert canonic Minuets, Haydn, Gurre-Lieder closing chorus.
8. Fugatos in *Eroica*, Ninth Symphony, *Hammerklavier* Sonata, String Quartet Op. 59, No. 2, by Beethoven.
9. Combination of two or three parts as in Beethoven Quartet Op. 59, No. 2, Brahms String Quartet in B♭ (3rd movement), Schoenberg First Quartet.
10. Imitations—Mozart String Quartet in G, etc.

GLOSSARY

Original usage	*Equivalent English usage*
whole note	semibreve
half note	minim
quarter note	crotchet
eighth note	quaver
tone	note
tonality	key
substitute tones	altered, 'raised' 6th and 7th notes of minor
mixed notes	mixed note values
degree (as V or VII)	(i) chord built on a degree of a scale
	(ii) step in a scale when related to another step in that scale
measure (ms.)	bar
prime	unison
cross relation	false relation
voice leading (or part leading)	part writing
open parallels (8s or 5s)	consecutive octaves or fifths
hidden parallels	hidden octaves or fifths
intermittent parallels	non-consecutive octaves or fifths
authentic cadence	perfect cadence
deceptive cadence (or progression)	interrupted cadence
− (dim.)	diminished (interval)
+ (aug.)	augmented (interval)
6-chord	6/3 chord

INDEX

(References are to page numbers)